KAMCHATKA
Land of Fire and Ice

KAMCHATKA
Land of Fire and Ice

Vadim Gippenreiter
with an introduction by
Robert Perkins

LAURENCE KING

Published 1992 by
Laurence King Publishing

Copyright © 1992 Photographs
and text by Vadim Gippenreiter
© 1992 Introduction by Robert
Perkins

A catalogue record for this book is
available from the British Library

ISBN 1 85669 020 2

Translated by James Paver
and Dr Arch Tait
Designed by Mikhail Anikst
Typeset by Upstream,
High Wycombe
Printed in Singapore by Toppan

Frontispiece
View of the Tolbachik eruption,
1975.

Contents

Introduction

There are few places left in the world whose names cannot immediately be recognized. Kamchatka is one of them. To most Europeans and Americans the name is exotic, the place unknown, but for those aware of it, the Kamchatka peninsula has always been alluring.

I first heard of Kamchatka as a teenager, playing a board game called *Risk*. The game suited the political climate of the 1950s: by rolling dice on a world map, and massing my armies (represented by painted wooden cubes) I could, if I was lucky, beat my brother and sisters in a contest for global domination. To invade America directly from the Soviet Union I had to have this oddly shaped piece of Russia called Kamchatka.

Our games reflected the fact that Kamchatka used to form one of the most impenetrable borders in the world. As part of Russia's closest border to the United States, and containing her largest ice-free port, its strategic value outweighed any other consideration, and for generations it has been surrounded by secrecy, as has the whole of the Soviet Far East. As recently as 1983, a Korean Airlines jumbo jet was shot down over Sakhalin Island for invading Soviet air space in this sensitive area. Since the turbulent changes in Russia in 1990, the future is even less clear. It is possible that new political and economic structures may help to reverse Kamchatka's role and make her the gateway to opportunity instead of a closed border.

In 1988 I met the Russian journalist Vasily Peskov, who wished to write a book about Alaska. Vasily was especially interested in the problems of conservation and the dilemmas of the native people in America and the Soviet Union. In return, even though it was a closed zone, I suggested a visit to the Kamchatka peninsula.

I had encountered the name of Kamchatka again in a book called *Tent Life in Siberia* written in the 1860s by George Kennan, and this had rekindled my interest. Kennan was twenty years old when he sailed from San Francisco to Kamchatka in 1864 as part of a three-man advance team working for the Western Union Telegraph company. He and his companions spent three years in Siberia, hiring workers, mapping the route, and preparing for the work to begin, and his book survives as one of the great nineteenth-century travelogues. Other works I read at the time included *Journal of a Voyage with Bering, 1741-1742* by Georg Wilhelm Steller, John Ledyard's *Journey Through Russia and Siberia, 1787-1788, The History of Kamchatka* by S. P. Krasheninnikov and *Physical Geography of Asiatic Russia* by S. P. Suslov. These books described an exotic land, full of volcanoes, and with an impressive native cultural history. The Soviet Encyclopedia of Geographic Terms defines Kamchatka thus '. . . a peninsula in Northeast Asia. Its shores are washed by the Pacific Ocean, the Sea of Okhotsk and the Bering Sea. The peninsula extends for 1,200 km and has a width of up to 450 km. Its area is equal to 37,000 square km. The central part of the peninsula is crossed by two ranges –

Avacha Bay, Kamchatka.
Early engraving.

Sredinnyi Khrebet (Middle Range) and Vostochnyi Khrebet (Eastern Range). The Central-Kamchatka lowland lies between them, and the Kamchatka River flows through it. There are more than 160 volcanoes on Kamchatka, about 30 of which are active.'

Eleven time zones from Moscow, Kamchatka is one of the farthest outposts of the Soviet Union. Although its major city, Petropavlovsk, was an active, international seaport under the Czars, no foreigner had been allowed to travel in Kamchatka for fifty years until Vasily obtained permission for our visit in 1990. Over our seven-week visit, we saw much of the diversity of Kamchatka's topography, and met fishermen, politicians, archaeologists, hunters, reindeer herders, conservationists, artists, scientists, housewives and soldiers. Few of the people we met had previously talked to Americans, and to them our presence was a sure sign that the times were changing. They were as eager for change as they were nervous about how it would affect them. They talked openly about their fears and hopes, their lives and the system under which they lived.

Kamchatka came late to the Russian Empire; it was annexed by the Cossacks only in 1697. Although Russian history had portrayed this as a 'free display of the brotherly spirit of Great Russians', whose movement 'toward the Sun' was inspired only by a thirst for knowledge, it was equally the story of forced and bloody subjugation of native cultures, not unlike the westward march of Europeans across North America.

Before the conquest of the peninsula there were approximately two hundred permanent native settlements. Atlasov, a Cossack chief, wrote in 1701 that before their arrival between one hundred and fifty and two hundred people lived in every Koryak *ostrozek,* or small fort, and up to five hundred and more in the Itelmen settlements along the Kamchatka River. Today these native peoples, the Itelmeny, Koryaky, Chukchi and Eveny, make up only two-and-a-half per cent of the population.

Georg Steller, the naturalist accompanying Vitus Bering, wrote in his *Beschreibung von dem Lande Kamschatka* that after Russia gained control of Kamchatka, 'the Cossacks in forty years reduced the number of natives to one-twelfth or even to one-fifteenth of the original population'. Between one-hundred-and-thirty thousand and one-hundred-and-fifty thousand native people were reduced to ten thousand. There were a number of unsuccessful rebellions against Russian rule. One of the most famous was led by Feodor Khurchin in 1731, and its failure was followed by a mass suicide by the indigenous people, who preferred death to captivity.

The eastward expansion of the Russian Empire had been fuelled by the pursuit of sable. Until the Russians' arrival, Kamchatka's inhabitants did not value sable fur, although Atlasov recorded that the Itelmeny caught a few, 'not for the use of the skins, because those were considered worse than dog skins, but for the meat, which they used as food'. Sable tails were also mixed with clay to make pots, and sable bones were used to make needles.

View of Petropavlovsk.
Early engraving.

Sable has long been a valued currency in Russia, whether under the Great Princes, the Czars, the Imperial Court or the Soviets. The result of this quest was similar to that of the European fur trade's expansion across Canada in pursuit of beaver, which brought in its wake religion, settlers and disease. Both expansions had disastrous results for the native populations, both animal and human.

A trade monopoly on sable was introduced during the reign of Peter the Great (1701-1725). After 1922 this became a state monopoly, which was extended by the Soviets to include the other great native resource of Kamchatka, the salmon.

Russian traders had no commercial interest in salmon until 1896. Before then they caught the fish as the native people did, to feed themselves and their dogs, but after the first salmon processing factory was established at the mouth of the Kamchatka River, the site of the peninsula's most concentrated salmon run, this resource became increasingly controlled. The Japanese were the major buyers of the cured fish and sponsored the building of the factory. Ostensibly renting both the factory and the river, they used their own boats and workers to harvest the salmon, an arrangement that lasted until the outbreak of the Second World War.

Up until 1930, anyone could catch salmon for himself with no limit. The imposition of limits, culminating in 1960 in an allowance of sixty kilos of salmon per year for a native, meant that native dog teams died out because the dogs could not be fed, and severely affected winter transportation which was primarily by dogsled. Each man's team represented an important part of his livelihood and without them natives were restricted to travelling and hunting closer to home. Today, increasing interest in dog team competitions is slowly bringing dogsleds back to Kamchatka.

Karl von Ditmar, one of Kamchatka's explorers in the 1850s, wrote: 'Animal life at the mouths of Kamchatka's rivers is enormously rich. The main condition favouring this variety is an incredible amount of salmon, annually entering the rivers from the sea, and even into the outermost creeks, often located in high mountains, where this fish amasses along the banks. With the coming of the fish into the rivers, the life on this land renews. After salmon, big groups of seals come into the rivers and lakes . . . Like people, different animals – bears, wolves, sled dogs, foxes – constantly stay near the streams. A multitude of geese, ducks, loons, swans fill up the air and the surface of the waters. In the late fall it becomes more quiet, and in the winter voices of birds and animals cease. Inhabitants, who haven't stored enough *yukola* [sun-dried fish], starve in the winter time, because the land, just recently teeming with life, is totally dead.'

Salmon and sable are the primary cash crops for the peninsula. In the three hundred years since its conquest, the total salmon catch has increased fifty times, from thirty thousand tons to nearly one-and-a-half million tons a year. Moscow buys the salmon and sable to sell on the international market. There is

Above
Kamchatkan natives preparing
yukola (dried fish) for the winter.
Early engraving.

Below
View of a typical Kamchatkan village
in the late eighteenth century.
Early engraving.

a traditional resentment towards Moscow, and the Kamchatka cooperatives are impatient to sell directly to the international market and realize a higher profit for their furs and fish. Foreign investment is already reappearing on the peninsula, with Japanese as well as European and American companies forming joint ventures to modernize not only the salmon fishery, but the crab, timber, and hunting activities on the peninsula.

We landed in Petropavlovsk on 19 July 1990. Vitus Bering, who spent years in Kamchatka preparing for his Pacific expedition of discovery, founded the city in 1740, and named it after his two packet ships, the *St Peter* and the *St Paul*. Actually, there are two Petropavlovsks, a civilian one with three hundred and fifty thousand inhabitants, and a military one on the western bank of Avacha Bay with an equal number of inhabitants, which harbours the Pacific submarine fleet, as well as a major naval base. Military personnel usually stay three years before being transferred to less remote posts. Civilian workers on the peninsula have traditionally received a higher wage than their equals in less remote parts of the Soviet Union and usually leave Kamchatka once they have saved enough money.

Avacha Bay is one of the largest and best protected natural harbours in the world, although generations of military dumping of fuel, oil and even radioactive waste have polluted the water. This doesn't stop the citizens of Petropavlovsk from lining the banks of the Avacha River to fish. We watched hundreds of people fishing with whatever homemade net, hand-line or rod they could put together. Can there be a major city anywhere else in the world, where a salmon run exists half-an-hour from the centre?

Petropavlovsk sprawls over the hills and sits in the valleys surrounding Avacha Bay, sleepy and self-contained, waiting for the change that will come as Russia opens itself to the West. However, the arrival of news from the West has not always been so welcome. On Nikolskaya Sopka, one of the hills overlooking the bay, stands a war memorial. During the Crimean War (1853-1856) England and France joined forces with the Ottoman Turks in sending a combined fleet to capture Petropavlovsk. The official Imperial Manifesto announcing the war was received at the small church in the governor's town on 1 October 1854. The ship's messenger who delivered the news was shocked by the laughter and merriment it provoked among the parishioners – because it was arriving half a year too late.

In March 1854 an American whaler had reached Kamchatka from Honolulu, bearing a letter from the King of the Sandwich Islands to Kamchatka's governor, alerting him to the possibility of attack by a combined English-French fleet. Since Petropavlovsk was far removed from Europe, and its inhabitants had heard nothing of the Crimean War, an attack seemed unlikely. Luckily, the small garrison prepared to defend the town in any case, although it was felt their preparations would be for nothing.

P. Semenov-Tijnshansky, leader of the 1908-10 Kamchatka expedition. Financed by the Ryabushinsky family, rich Moscow merchants, the expedition's objective was geological discovery.

On 18 August, an English-French fleet did sail into Avacha Bay. There were five ships and one steamer that immediately opened fire with 220 naval cannon. They expected to stun an unsuspecting Petropavlovsk into submission, but the six coastal artillery batteries that replied surprised the attackers and killed the admiral of the English squadron, Sir David Price. The battle lasted several days, and between the 20th and the 24th the allies attempted to land troops, but were repelled. Karl von Ditmar, the explorer and one of the defenders of Petropavlovsk, wrote: 'The Kamchadls meted out deadly bullets from their little rifles. They are excellent hunters, who calculate each shot. They told later how they looked for a chance to shoot in such a manner that they would pierce with one bullet two enemies, who were standing one behind the other. This they called "pairing".' By 27 August the attack was over. The undermanned and underarmed garrison had defeated the best that Europe could throw against them.

Nearly one hundred and forty years later, I spent the summer travelling among the natural wonders of the peninsula, the most dramatic and stunning of which are its volcanoes. From our first day we felt their presence when we saw the three peaks of Koryak, Avacha and Kozelsky towering above Petropavlovsk. As Vadim Gippenreiter's powerful photographs show, of Kamchatka's 160 volcanoes, 30 are still active today.

The native peoples of Kamchatka once held that volcanic eruptions were caused when the spirits who lived in the volcanoes were disturbed, and preferred never to approach them. Today, these spectacular upheavals of the earth's magma attract rather than repel visitors. In the summer the Olympic ski team practises high up on the volcano snow fields, and people hike constantly on and around them. We climbed Avacha, a 2,738-metre-high volcano, the day after we arrived. We were lucky with the weather; there were no clouds, and the view stretched out across the ocean on our left, to the Koryak volcano on our right and into the valley beneath us, shimmering in the purple heat of a July afternoon.

Kamchatka lies along the Pacific volcanic rim and is a northern continuation of the Kurile volcanic chain. A second volcanic arc extends eastward from Kamchatka through the Aleutian Islands. Arranged primarily in groups or rings on the high plateaus around the centres of earlier eruptions, these beautiful, sharp-pointed volcanic peaks are scattered from the southern tip of the peninsula to Mount Shiveluch at 57 degrees north latitude. They give the eastern region of Kamchatka a unique landscape.

Eruptions of some of the Kamchatka volcanoes have been like those of Mount Etna in Sicily, relatively quiet outpourings of lava. Others, like those photographed for this book, have been violent explosions that eject huge quantities of debris and volcanic ash. The most powerful eruption occurred in 1907 when Mount Shtyubelya demolished the bottom of its crater and volcanic ash was expelled with enough force to cover the whole peninsula. So much

Above
Chukchi people with a typical nomadic shelter. Early twentieth century.

Below
Koryak shelter. A frame for drying animal skins and fish can be seen in the background. Early twentieth century.

Kamchatkan native photographed
in 1895.

Contemporary Kamchatkan woman
in traditional dress.

ash was suspended in the air that in Petropavlovsk lighted windows could not be seen from across the street.

Kamchatka also boasts the Kronotsky Nature Reserve, an area of more than a million hectares, whose natural beauty has been recognized since the time of the Czars. The Soviets made it into a national park, with this difference from those found elsewhere in the world: it is off-limits for development of any kind, and is used exclusively for scientific research, although the possibility of limited tourism is being explored. The journey to the reserve was made in a large transport helicopter capable of carrying two dozen people and hundreds of pounds of equipment and goods. We sat among crates of fresh eggs, bags of garlic and sacks of potatoes. It was clear that the food shortages plaguing the major Russian cities were not present in Kamchatka. Everyone had enough.

The pilot flew over one unpopulated valley after another, sometimes unnervingly low, so that we looked across at the trees growing up the sides of the valleys rather than upon them. The copilot threw open the side door at one point to allow us to get a better view. The Uzon Caldera opened before us, a huge plateau surrounded by ragged mountains which formed the rim of a volcano thousands of years ago. Upon landing we realized that the unloading was to be done without shutting the helicopter's rotary blades off, and our guide had to motion us to lie on top of our packs and food boxes as the helicopter left. When the roar of the engine faded we found ourselves in a field of ripe blueberries. Our camp was set up among some nearby juniper bushes, taking advantage of their great sprays of thick cover as protection from the wind.

The variety of volcanic phenomena was exceptional. The lakes smoked; there were large and small clay holes that bubbled, steamed or burped. More than sixty groups of hot springs are located in Kamchatka's districts with past or present volcanic activity. Their density near active or recently active volcanoes indicates that they are connected to magmatic centres lying close to the surface beneath the extinct volcanoes. Hot springs are the last manifestation of volcanic activity.

A copse of birch trees, with gnarled limbs and of diminutive stature added to the surreal quality of the landscape. The walking was wet, and we drew our drinking water from one of the many streams. Nearby the cabin that had marked our landing strip was a large porcelain-coloured pond of hot water where we bathed, trying not to sit or step on the jets of scalding water feeding it. Rubbing one's skin clean with the gritty volcanic mud was surprisingly enjoyable.

Another of Kamchatka's extraordinary natural phenomena is the Valley of Geysers, which was a day's walk from our camp. We followed the river flowing out of the Caldera, then a small stream that led us through rolling hills to the top of a divide, where sat a stone cairn. Our guide told us that every hiker added a stone before entering the valley and we dutifully added ours.

19

Members of the Russian expedition
to Kamchatka of 1895.

Our walk down took place in lengthening shadows, through grasses and weeds that stood chest high. Hundreds of small spiders floating on thin strands of web were riding the wind. The air became cooler, the descent steeper. Finally, we entered the valley.

The Valley of Geysers was discovered by chance by a geologist, Tatyana Ustinova, in 1941. It is in the reserve south of Lake Kronotskoye, near Uzon and Kikhpinich peaks. Through the valley flows Geyzernoy Creek, where the water of the hot springs and geysers escapes with a rush from holes that range in diameter from less than an inch to more than a yard. The jets are accompanied by steam and spray and strange sounds that blend with the continuous rumble of the overflowing water.

Walking there on my own I had the feeling of a traveller in Yellowstone Park during the 1880s, not the 1990s, with no hot-dog stands or car parks, although the largest geyser, Velikan, is equal to Yellowstone's Old Faithful, hurling a column of boiling water and steam fifty metres in the air. Other geysers throw forth intermittent jets of heated water and steam. The sulphur deposits built up on the rocks around them are very colourful – browns, yellows, and greens in tones not often seen in nature. Each geyser also has geyserettes of its own form and colour, depending on the chemical composition of the water, the thermophilic algae and various other micro-organisms that dwell in them. Above the main group of geysers on the upper platforms of the valley are mud holes of fine clay which gurgle and sigh. The landscape runs riot with multiple colours, dips and hollows as though a magnificent soufflé had become a gigantic flop, leaving in its wake this vivid, wrinkled, smoking masterpiece.

There are oil and natural gas deposits inside the Kronotsky Reserve, but they have not been developed. Not even hunters can enter it. One man told me how his dogs chased a bear into the reserve, forcing him to wait three days at its border until they gave up the chase and returned to him. One of our fellow hikers was a retired oil geologist, who had returned to the valley to continue his research. His conclusion after a lifetime of scientific thought was: 'The more I study nature, the more I wish to preserve her'.

This sentiment was echoed again and again by the people we met. Not only in the reserve, but in all parts of the peninsula, people share a sense of urgency about preserving nature. Unlike other parts of the far eastern republics, Kamchatka is not yet heavily industrialized. Much of its natural beauty remains intact. Its people are afraid that the opening of their country to a free market system will erode the natural resources and turn areas like the Kronotsky Reserve into huge tourist developments or, worse, playgrounds for industry. Many of the residents of Kamchatka are determined not to allow this to happen. Several years ago a river near the reserve, the Zhupanova, would have been dammed for hydroelectric power without the persevering opposition of the local people. The Water Development Office for Kamchatka is in

Man of the Kamchatkan Nanai tribe.

St Petersburg, eleven time zones away. Without local consultation the engineers and the first pieces of heavy equipment arrived in Kamchatka and made their way towards the river. As soon as the people understood what was happening, they took action. Among them was the head of the Fishing and Hunting Cooperative with which we were staying. The Zhupanova happened to be one of the rivers in his care. If it were dammed, he knew the salmon run would end and the animals that depended on them would disappear. This would hurt his business, of course, but he also cared about the ecological damage which would result. He had come to the peninsula decades before because Kamchatka is the furthest one can get from the centres of power, Moscow and St Petersburg. As he said, it attracts people of independent spirit, people who want to be a little more free.

With several of his men, he flew to meet the small convoy. While he talked to the engineers, his men disconnected the starter motors from the trucks and quietly loaded them into the helicopter. When the helicopter left, so did the starters. This gave the boss and the other concerned citizens time to talk with the planners in St Petersburg to see if they really meant to destroy the river. Fortunately for the salmon and for the Cooperative, the planners changed their collective mind.

North of Telichiki, in the tundra, live the reindeer herders. From April or May until the first snowfall they live a nomadic life grazing their herds of reindeer, most returning to spend the winter months in a village, except for the few herdsmen who stay with the deer. Each family owns just enough deer to supply its needs, but the majority of the animals belong to the government.

Reindeer antlers are another lucrative cash crop for Kamchatka, along with sable and salmon. The antlers are sold to the Asian medical markets, where they are believed to be capable of curing numerous ills. The herding tradition of the Eveny, Koryak and Chukchi peoples remains unbroken although the size of their herds has diminished. This long-lasting connection with the spiritual and practical focus of their life gives them a pride not present, for example, among some native groups in North America who have been taken away from their former life and given little in return.

Our visit to Kamchatka had been at an historical turning point when its future and the future of Russia are unfolding in dramatic ways every day. Vasily and I touched on this unsettling question on the morning of our departure. Along with my enthusiasm for all I had seen, I voiced my concern about safeguarding its future. Vasily replied 'No one knows the future, Robert, but let me tell you a story: there were once two frogs who fell in a bowl of sour cream. One of the frogs said, "This is awful". It gave a few pathetic kicks and drowned. The other frog, having thought things over, began to kick its legs hard. It kicked its front feet, too, and turned the sour cream into butter and jumped free'. Vasily looked hard at me as he finished the story and said, 'Robert, the Russian people are like the second frog.'

Robert Perkins
1991

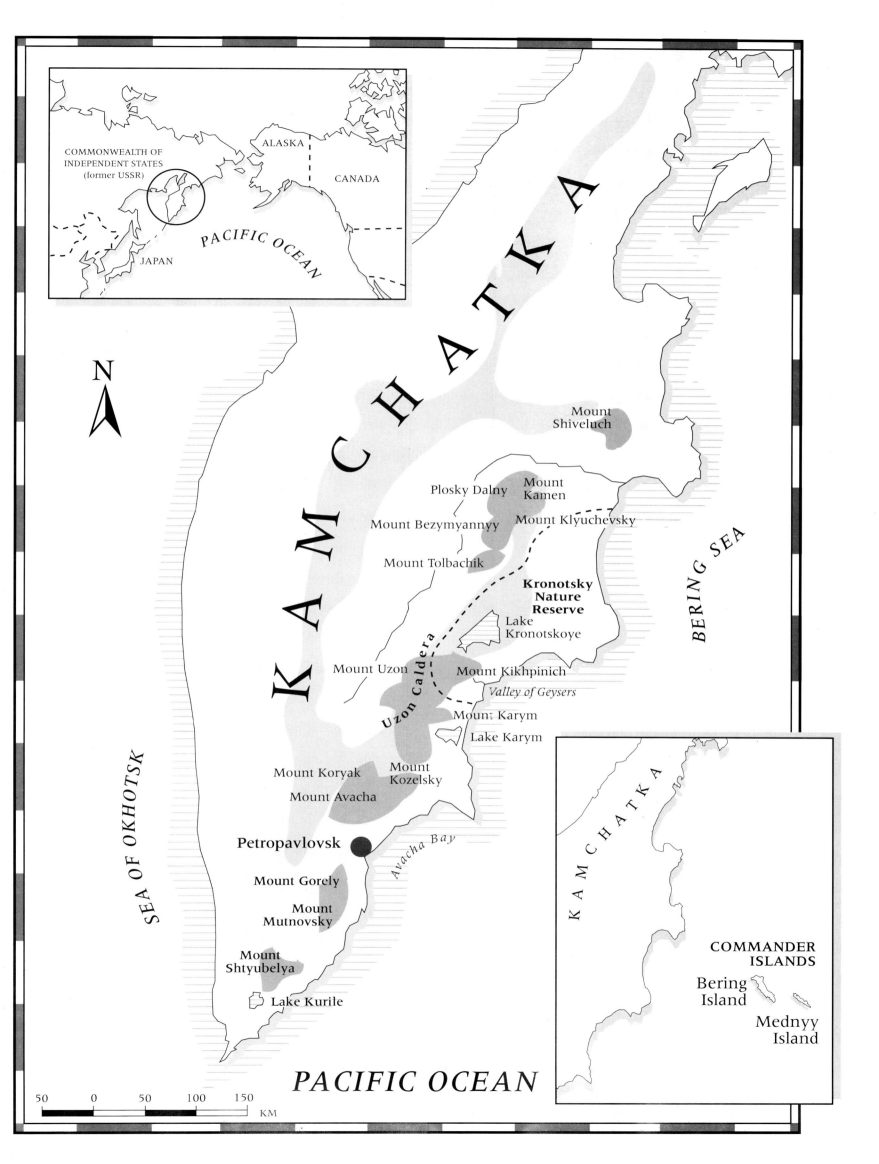

COMMONWEALTH OF
INDEPENDENT STATES
(former USSR)

ALASKA

CANADA

PACIFIC OCEAN

JAPAN

N

K A M C H A T K A

Mount
Shiveluch

Plosky Dalny   Mount
                 Kamen

Mount Bezymyannyy   Mount Klyuchevsky

Mount Tolbachik

Kronotsky
Nature
Reserve

Lake
Kronotskoye

BERING SEA

Mount Uzon   Mount Kikhpinich

Valley of Geysers

Uzon Caldera

Mount Karym

Lake Karym

Mount Koryak   Mount
                 Kozelsky

Mount Avacha

Petropavlovsk   ●

Avacha Bay

SEA OF OKHOTSK

Mount Gorely

Mount
Mutnovsky

Mount
Shtyubelya

Lake Kurile

K A M C H A T K A

COMMANDER
ISLANDS

Bering
Island

Mednyy
Island

PACIFIC OCEAN

50   0   50   100   150

KM

The Geological History of Kamchatka

In geological terms, Kamchatka is young. Its relief was formed less than a million years ago, during the Quaternary period, the most recent in the geological history of the planet. The sea floor rose and fractured and eruptions of basalt lava formed a huge plateau. The continued movement of the molten subterranean mass then broke up this platform and white-hot magma poured out of the fissures. The discharge of magma caused blocks to rise and fall and still more fissures appeared, which moulded the relief of the peninsula and formed the basis of its geological make-up. Further eruptions completed the formation of present day Kamchatka. Chains of volcanoes rose, adjacent to deep clefts; among them were the extraordinary volcanic peaks of Klyuchevsky, Shiveluch, Tolbachik, Koryak and Avacha. More than half of Kamchatka is covered with the results of volcanic eruptions.

The line of volcanoes on Kamchatka follows the same fault which runs through the volcanic ridge of the Kurile and Aleutian Islands. They are linked by a deep rift along which the continental shelves move against each other at the bottom of the ocean. At this loggerhead runs a trench, some 12,000 metres deep (the average depth of the ocean is 5,000 metres). This hollow, deep under water at the base of the arc of the islands and along the eastern shore of the narrow strip of Kamchatka, borders on the chain of volcanoes.

The surface membrane of the planet – the Earth's crust – is composed of a layer of hard rock, between sixty and seventy kilometres deep, separated by fractures into a series of plates. As a result of intense heat and shifts in the core of the planet, these move against each other. The most noticeable effects of this are seen where the plates meet. There are no gaps between them: if they move apart, molten rock is forced up from beneath to fill the space. When plates on the ocean floor move, one of them will be forced downwards beneath the other at such an angle as to form a deep trough or trench. Such plate movements cause intense focused tremors, and the combined effects of pressure and friction on the underside of the trench result in the formation of volcanoes.

Left
Mount Avacha, an active volcano, 2,738 metres in height, and thirty kilometres from the town of Petropavlovsk. A young cone is rising above the semicircle of an old caldera. In the foreground are lava flows from recent eruptions. Tourist groups often venture up to the crater, and vulcanologists carry out tests there.

Overleaf
The Klyuchevsky eruption. Although it is daylight, the air is darkened by dust and ash.

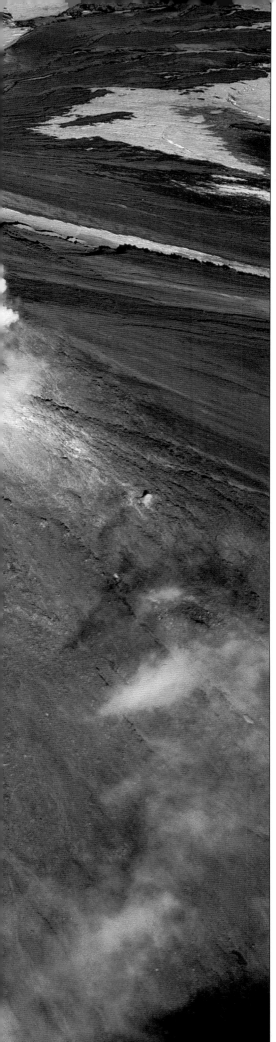

In Kamchatka and on the Kurile Islands there are sixty-eight 'young' volcanoes, which make up ten per cent of all the active volcanoes in the world. The volcanoes of Kamchatka are grouped in four separate chains. The westernmost is the oldest: these are extinct volcanoes of varying ages. Especially noteworthy are Khangar and Ichinsky. Their previous stages of activity are clearly visible – lava flows, craters, cinder cones and extrusions. The central Kamchatka lowland forms a vast depression between the central and eastern mountain ranges. Here are the volcanoes of the Klyuchevsky group and the volcano Shiveluch. Into the valley flows the greatest river on the peninsula – the Kamchatka – and its tributaries. The youngest volcanoes run along the Pacific coast of the peninsula: the eastern Kamchatka range. It begins with the volcanoes in the Gamchensk group, and ends with the volcanoes Koryak and Avacha in the south. The southern Kamchatka range is separated from the eastern by the width of Avacha Bay, which runs west to east, dividing lower Kamchatka from the rest. This chain continues south among the Kurile Islands.

It is common to link eruptions with earthquakes when talking of the natural disasters which strike the Pacific Rim. Although eruptions frequently take place without earthquakes, and earthquakes can occur where there are no volcanoes, Kamchatka and the Kurile Islands are regions where volcanic activity and earthquakes are closely related.

29

Left
The crater of Avacha was for many years a 'home laboratory' for vulcanologists. It offers many examples of post-volcanic activity. It erupted as recently as spring 1991. The crater is filled to the rim with lava, and small lava flows trickle down the outer slopes of the cone.

Overleaf
Mounts Kamen and Klyuchevsky. The volcanoes of the Klyuchevsky group rise up from an ancient shield plateau, ninety kilometres in diameter. Kamen is extinct but Klyuchevsky is still very active. It erupts both from the crater at its summit and from the radial fissures at various altitudes on its slopes. During the eruptions of 1990 and 1991 the crater filled with lava, and a cinder cone formed on the surface. Magma was found at a depth of forty kilometres, filling an underground watercourse, while the main magma core was estimated to be as far down as 170 kilometres.

Earthquakes on the east coast of Kamchatka in the underwater trench take place at a relatively shallow depth. The most active earthquake zone lies between the eastern volcanic chain and the trench. The earthquakes on the eastern coast of the peninsula and on the Kurile Islands occur within an area about 150 kilometres wide and are among the most powerful on the planet.

Volcanic eruptions and their accompanying phenomena are spread all around the 'ring of fire' which encircles the Pacific Ocean. During an eruption a vast quantity of red-hot matter is scattered over the surrounding region, accompanied by jets of steam, gases and salts which are highly soluble in water. The rock and ash which are spewed out in an eruption are washed down in streams and rivers and settle on the beds of seas and oceans. Big eruptions involve very high-temperature volcanic activity, which produces sulphuric, hydrochloric and other acids. Useful minerals are produced in the form of ore deposits. Others are washed into the ocean, forming sedimentary rocks, clay, soluble silicates and calcium compounds.

Volcanoes define the natural appearance of Kamchatka. Valleys are formed by layers of ash and cinders, criss-crossed by a network of 'dry rivers' – channels filled only during the spring thaw or after heavy rain. The slopes of the volcanoes are cut by barrancas – sharp ridges, alternating with deep troughs – the result of water and wind erosion, and abrupt falls in temperature.

32

Right
Mount Koryak

Overleaf
Mount Kambalny (2,160 metres) and
Mount Kosheleva (1,863 metres).
Active volcanoes lying in the south of
Kamchatka. Nowadays their activity
shows itself in the form of mighty
fumaroles and very hot springs.

Following spread
Bolshaya Udina, an extinct volcano.

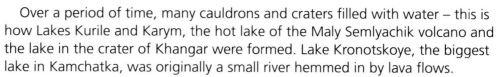

Over a period of time, many cauldrons and craters filled with water – this is how Lakes Kurile and Karym, the hot lake of the Maly Semlyachik volcano and the lake in the crater of Khangar were formed. Lake Kronotskoye, the biggest lake in Kamchatka, was originally a small river hemmed in by lava flows.

The climate around the coast of Kamchatka is damp, with heavy snowfalls, thick fog, rain and strong winds; inland it is dryer and much more continental. The great height of the mountainous massifs and volcanoes, combined with such a damp climate, has led to the formation of glaciers. These glaciers and snowfields are the sources of Kamchatka's rivers, and in the clean and fast-running waters salmon spawn in vast numbers. Hot volcanic debris ensures the presence of geysers, hot lakes and warm rivers. From the wide lowlands of western Kamchatka to the peaks of the volcanoes and mountain ranges one can trace sheer lines of vegetation.

Volcanic ash is extraordinarily fertile: the marshland and tundra of the coastal terraces give way to forests of fir and spruce, which in turn give way to deciduous forests, while the stony slopes are covered with birch, undergrowth and tall grass. Alder trees, clinging to the heights, are supplanted by lichen-covered tundra with dark patches of small, windbeaten cedars and squat, low bushes hugging the rock face, interspersed with alpine meadows. On the heights only the very hardiest of plants cling to the rock face and bare scree, exposed to the worst of the foul weather.

39

The Kronotsky Reserve on Kamchatka is one of the largest nature reserves in the world, with an area of more than a million hectares. Access to the park is extremely difficult as it is far from any village or settlement and is almost entirely free of any man-created influences. Perhaps more than any other area on Kamchatka, the park represents the unique quality of the peninsula; all the natural phenomena of the region are represented within its boundaries.

Left
The caldera on Ksudach. At the summit of this huge shield volcano are several lakes, filling craters resulting from explosions. In the centre background is the young crater, Shtyubelya.

Overleaf
Mount Karym. Situated in the centre of the eastern volcanic range, 1,486 metres in height and one of the most active volcanoes in Kamchatka. Explosive eruptions occur periodically, one after another, with outpourings of lava from the central crater. The height of the cone from the bottom of the caldera measures five hundred metres, and it is easily accessible to any visitor.

Mount Khangar, located in the south
of the middle Kamchatka volcanic
range. A lake has formed in the
collapsed summit which is 150 metres
deep in its centre.

Above
Mount Karym. One of the most
active volcanoes in Kamchatka, in the
centre of the eastern volcanic range.
The caldera in the foreground of the
picture is three-and-a-half kilometres
in diameter.

Overleaf
View across the Bering Sea from the
shores of Kamchatka.

The Giants of Kamchatka

The immense size of the volcanoes of Kamchatka can only be appreciated fully from the air. Prominent among them is the Klyuchevsky group, the most active segment of the Kurilo-Kamchatka arc. Twelve volcanoes lie on the same volcanic foundation, covering a total of eight-and-a-half thousand square metres. The history of volcanic activity in the peninsula can be read in the thick layers of volcanic rock.

The oldest volcanoes of the Klyuchevsky group are Plosky Dalny, Kamen, Udina, Zimina and Tolbachik. Klyuchevsky, Bezymyannyy, Shiveluch and Tolbachik are still active; the others in the group are extinct. Volcanic activity in the area lasted for many thousands of years, gradually smothering the sharper volcanic formations with successive layers of lava. The broad crater at the summit of Plosky Dalny is now filled by a glacier, and only some gentle fumaroles, the vents through which hot gases escape, provide evidence of its former volatility. The geological history of Mount Kamen is also easy to read – after the mighty eruption which destroyed half of the cone, the south face is almost completely vertical, with ridges and layers of ancient lava.

The largest glaciers in Kamchatka formed on the peaks and slopes of volcanoes during the Ice Age which coincided with greatly increased volcanic activity. Mount Bezymyannyy rose up on the slopes of Mount Kamen. At the same time a basalt strato-volcano began to grow, later to form Mount Klyuchevsky, and Mount Shiveluch rose up on the left bank of the River Kamchatka at the intersection of two plates, the Kurilo-Kamchatka and Aleutian Island arcs.

Left
Mount Kamen, an extinct, destroyed volcano, is on the right. Mount Klyuchevsky can be seen beyond it.

Overleaf
Volcanoes in the Klyuchevsky group – Mounts Bezymyannyy, Kamen, Klyuchevsky and Plosky Dalny. On the outlying slopes at the foot of the mountains are lava streams and cinder cones from secondary eruptions.

50

Mount Bezymyannyy ('The Nameless One'). An unremarkable-looking mountain, 3,000 metres high, whose outward appearance gives no indication of its previous history. After several centuries of inactivity it had lost its volcanic appearance, hence its uncomplimentary name. Moreover, it lies at the foot of the ruined and extinct Kamen, and alongside the giant Klyuchevsky. In general it had never done anything to demand attention, but in 1955 and 1956 this featureless mountain underwent dramatic changes: earthquakes started and its outline began to change and to swell up on one side. The tremors were followed by heavy falls of ash and gas. The main eruption happened at 5.11pm on 30 March 1956. An observer in the nearby settlement of Klyuchi recorded that the height of the ash cloud was estimated at about thirty-eight kilometres: 'The site of the eruption could not be seen. The ash cloud headed towards the settlement, accompanied by endless flashes of lightning and the growing roar of thunder. The ash fall started. The gloom was so impenetrable that it was impossible to see your hand in front of your face. People returning from work blundered around the settlement looking for their homes. The air was full of electricity. Telephones rang spontaneously, radio transmitters fused. There was a strong smell of sulphur . . . A great mass of ash was thrown into the atmosphere and was taken by air currents . . . on 1 April it was sighted in Alaska . . . and on 3 April it was seen over the British Isles at a height of fifteen kilometres. The visible evidence of this massive eruption was on a vast scale, exceeding by far anything that even the oldest inhabitants of Kamchatka had ever seen.'

Twenty-five kilometres away strong trees were snapped and flattened by the force of the explosion. Scorching hot debris covered an area of five hundred square kilometres and a fierce thaw set in. Muddy streams flooded, throwing down great stones and smashing all before them. The small River Khapitsa washed down masses of rock thrown out by explosions – even now, for a distance of fifteen kilometres, its banks are walls twenty metres high. In the lower reaches of the river were ice boulders weighing hundreds of tons, carried down by the force of the water.

The explosion destroyed the whole of the eastern half of the volcano. Instead of the cone shape there was a huge crater, open to the south, and at its centre an extruded cupola of magma was rising up from great depths, heated to a temperature of a thousand degrees. The pent-up energy inside this cupola was immense. Its slow growth triggered new explosions, sending scorching avalanches pouring down the slopes. At night red-hot lava glowed in the gaping fissures. A constant hail of rocks rained down from the cupola and from the walls surrounding it. Bezymyannyy lies in a deserted wilderness. The settlement of Klyuchi is shielded from it by Kamen and Klyuchevsky, so there were no casualties during the eruption. The desert created by the eruption is coming back to life now. Shoots of alder and silver birch are sprouting through the layers of ash, and rosebay willowherb is flowering. Partridges have returned and there are tracks left by hares.

The expanding cupola is gradually filling the funnel left by the eruption. The top is now approaching the level of the surrounding walls. The seepage of molten lava continues as a result of periodic explosions, less powerful, but still preventing the construction of a permanent base in the crater.

In the distance, behind Bezymyannyy, loom the massive volcanoes of Ostry and Plosky Tolbachik.

Mount Klyuchevsky is a great work of nature, forming a link between two separate groups of volcanoes which lie on a broad lava substructure. Besides the eruptions from the summit, fissure eruptions also occur on its slopes. Lava breaches have developed at various heights right down to the foot of the volcano, in a series of radial fissures. Powerful secondary eruptions occur periodically, forming lava flows and cinder cones. Hundreds of the latter may be seen all around the volcano. Klyuchevsky has long been a focus of attention for travellers and scientists visiting Kamchatka. Daniil Gauss, a member of Billings' expedition, was the first to reach the summit in 1788. There are no records of any further ascents until 1931. Between 1931 and 1958 there were fifteen successful expeditions to the summit, two of which ended in tragedy with the deaths of two men. The following chapter is an account of my own visit during the eruption of 1966.

52

Right
Large boulders and splintered rock thrown up by one of the many explosions from the extruded cupola on Bezymyannyy.

Overleaf
Looking upwards along the western face of Mount Shiveluch, the largest volcano in northern Kamchatka. Its short period of activity was particularly powerful, especially the great explosion in 1964, which was one of the largest eruptions of the twentieth century. Two square kilometres of solid rock were blown into the air and scattered in crumbs on the western face of the volcano. The flow of lava altered the relief of a wide area, killed off the plant life, and diverted the watercourses. A cupola of extruded magma began to rise slowly in the hollow left by the explosion.

The Klyuchevsky Eruption

Mount Klyuchevsky has always attracted attention. The highest point on Kamchatka, it is visible from everywhere on the peninsula. In the autumn of 1966, after a period of inactivity, it reawoke. A cloud of ash was permanently visible. On a starry night, lava spraying into the crater lit up the summit like a torch, five kilometres in the air. Seismographs placed at the foot of the volcano measured the level of activity.

In October 1966 the seismographs registered a series of earth tremors coming from the direction of Klyuchevsky. Their intensity indicated that a large eruption was due. The data enabled scientists to estimate the epicentre and probable time of the eruption. On the night of 6 November on the northern face at a height of two thousand metres, a radial fissure eight hundred metres long opened. The eruption had started – this was a lateral eruption of lava. A constant roar could be heard in the settlement of Klyuch, thirty kilometres away. A black cloud of ash, stones and gases was growing above the fountain of molten lava. It was a fantastic spectacle. Several funnel craters formed along the fissure. Soon the eruption focused in the centre of the fissure, a cinder cone began to form and lava seeped from its foot, filling the water channel which flowed down the valley.

In October at two thousand metres up a mountainside it is the middle of winter. Our expedition set up base camp seven kilometres from the site of the eruption. Horses and dogs were used to haul tents, firewood, provisions and scientific equipment up to the camp. While we were doing this, the lava advanced nine kilometres. For the vulcanologists in the party, this was the first full-scale eruption we had witnessed. Even a howling blizzard could not stop us from watching what was happening. That evening we struggled through snowdrifts and thickets to the edge of a gully. Far below was the bed of a dried-up river. A black mass of stones was slowly creeping forward, filling the gully. At its head a red belt of lava snaked along. It was accompanied by the crackling sound of cooling debris. When a sizeable lump broke away, the molten gold burst into flames, then slowly died down, glowing a yellow gold, then orange, then claret. We slid down the precipice until we were almost on top of this amazing sight. The lava moved on irresistibly, covering the gully with cooling rocks. The heat conductivity was so low that unmelted snow lay alongside; after an eruption, the centre of each rock keeps its heat for years.

The next day we climbed to the centre of the eruption. It was a long and difficult march. We had to haul our sleeping bags, tents, provisions, cameras and other equipment up the mountain. It was no use waiting for the helicopter because the weather was too poor for flying. Like ants on sand, we scuttled across the cooling rocks. Above us it seemed quieter than we had expected. It was like being on an icebreaker when the whole ice pack is moving: the landscape on either side slides by, and the ship appears to be standing still.

Mount Klyuchevsky. A secondary eruption which took place in 1966 and 1967. Molten lava can be seen gushing from the crater of the cinder cone and falling on the slopes of the volcano.

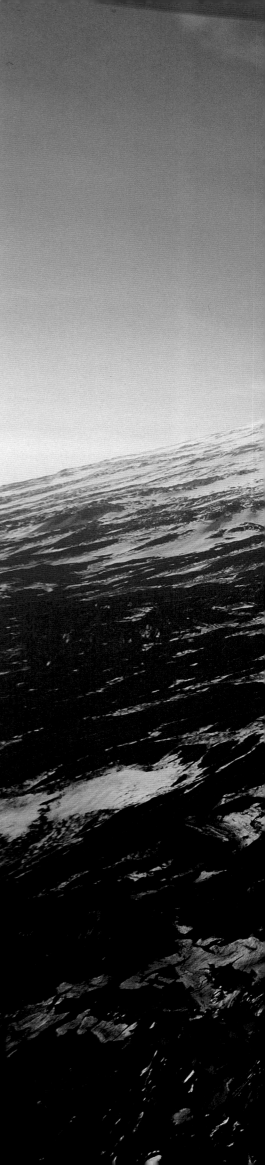

We were in a lead-coloured landscape where, even though it was winter, nothing white remained. The heat and the cold existed side by side. The sky was grey – heavy with dust and gases. The ash-laden gloom ate into the shadows, destroying any sense of height and depth. There was a strong smell of burning. We passed from rocky ground on to a covering of blackened snow, leaving white tracks stretching behind us. Heavy, dirty snow began to fall in the grey, uncertain light.

The lava flow had filled a wide valley, forcing its way down side gullies. In the swirl of the blizzard, red embers were slowly being extinguished. A black stormcloud dominated the summit of the volcano, obscuring its silhouette. Lightning flashed, the cracks of the thunder blending with the roar of the explosions. We were heading straight for the breach. The feeble rattle of a helicopter broke through the din of the eruption. It circled a couple of times but dared not risk a landing. After a day blundering around in this lead-coloured world, where grey ash clouds hovered around the mountain peak and clung to obelisks of rock, we ourselves had turned grey.

58 At last we reached our goal. Twilight reigned under a smoky canopy. Emerging from the valley, the lava flow flickered with light like a city at night. The stream ran with a rustling sound from the foot of the cinder cone into a vertically walled canyon. At its source it was bright, flowing lightly and quickly, then, lower down, it became wider and blacker, spreading to the sides and overflowing them. By this point it was moving barely perceptibly. A blue haze of gases trembled and played above the lava. One had the impression of watching the world's beginning, many millions of years ago.

Somewhere beyond the bounds of this world the sun was high in the sky, but the grey murk which enveloped us became even thicker. It pulsed and flowed with flashes of light, and echoed with sighs and thunder, so that we forgot altogether about the human world. The sulphur burst into blue tongues of flame. Higher up above the flow glowed the fiery mouth of the cinder cone. The swirling gases engulfed the lava and igneous fountains shot still higher, showering the black slopes of the cone. Somehow, in this inhuman environment, we had to find water and somewhere to pitch our camp. Naturally, there was no water here. The melted snow was poisonous with chemicals. After a long search we found clean snow in a deep drift. We cleared away the upper layers of stones with geological hammers to build a 'permanent' hearth in a depression in a stationary patch in the flow. The rocks were not red hot but the snow still melted. In one cooking pot we heated buckwheat, in the other coffee. The buckwheat was excellent, but the coffee was steel grey and smelled like a chemical factory. After supper, we headed back to the lava flow. The closer we got to the cinder cone, the greater was the likelihood of being hit on the head by a stone. To make matters worse, it was dark. But these worries faded against the prospect of being at the centre of events.

Finally we had to rest. We levelled the ground, spread our jackets and wet things on the hot boulders, put our inflatable mattresses on top of these and crawled into our sleeping bags. We tried hard to fall asleep, despite the heat below and the cold above. At about two in the morning our overheated mattresses collapsed. By three o'clock we were on our feet putting out our smouldering sleeping bags and jackets. The smells of the eruption mingled with those of burning rubber and fabric. Life beside the lava flow was difficult. Fragments of rock got into the cameras and grated in the mountings of the lenses. Put any cloth down, on even a slightly tepid stone, and its internal heat would begin to burn the material. Gases and dust stung our eyes. The skin on our hands and faces was like dried crocodile hide. The wind was either hot and full of gases and dust from the flow, or cold and full of dirty, acidic snow.

Insomnia is when you want to go to sleep but cannot. Here, on the mountain, we were ready to sleep at any moment, but nobody wanted to. It was impossible to cut yourself off from what was happening. We decided to build an 'isolation unit': we put up a tent in a depression in the snow, so that nothing of the landscape was visible. Within a few minutes a violent wind had torn it to shreds. We remained awake.

61

One day the helicopter made two passes, dropping planks, tents, firewood, a stove and supplies. We dug the tent in up to the roof and built an igloo-style entrance from snow bricks so that the wind could not blow in at the door. Damp and tired, but satisfied with our handiwork, we crawled inside. Then we had to go in search of water. The snow, even where it appeared to be clean, was bitter and acidic. As we clambered from one gully to another, a blizzard blew up, but we still managed to find a stream, which gave itself away by a quiet gurgling beneath thick snow at the bottom of a deep ravine. As night fell, the snowstorm got worse, blowing in off the Pacific. The gusts of wind were strong enough to shake coals out of the stove and to rattle the roof. Fine snow got into every nook and cranny. It melted against the stove but beyond the immediate heat it collected in miniature drifts. Silence fell around us: at first we could hear the explosions and the sound of the wind, but then all became quiet. We were completely covered by snow. It was extraordinary: we could even hear the candle spluttering, but faintly through the snow-covered roof of the tent we could also hear a growing roar. The eruption was continuing with increasing strength.

Lava river flowing from Mount Klyuchevsky at the height of the eruption.

62

Mount Klyuchevsky. General view of
the secondary eruption in 1966 and
1967. Lava is flowing out of an
underground watercourse at the foot
of the cinder cone.

The lava stream is moving away from
the foot of the cinder cone. Gas and
red hot rocks are erupting from a
crater on the cone.

We noticed a strict pattern – the eruption became stronger by night and decreased in strength by day. The worse the weather, the stronger the eruption, but in bright weather an idyllic calm reigned over the area. The fumarole was covered by mists, the crater by woolly white clouds.

At night, the snowstorms blew even harder above our heads. The snow was fluid. It did not form a solid covering above us, but slowly spread itself across the whole wasteland. The roof sagged increasingly. By our estimate there was about a ton of snow weighing down on just half of the roof and it would not last long under such weight. We slept with our heads towards the door in case of emergency. A single plank supported one side of the roof. The silence seemed to stretch out, then we heard a suspicious rustle. In the middle of the night we lit the stove and heated our breakfast, then crawled out to try to save the tent. We had to make a vertical tunnel with a stick through the snow to the air, and widen it with fists and spades. We crawled in and out like moles. Together we cleared the snow from the top of the tent.

We got out just in time. A plug of lava had formed in the valley so that the flow, instead of continuing gently downwards, was diverted towards us. The red wall was unhurriedly eating away the three hundred metres which lay between it and ourselves. As I ran before the lava, I saw the camp succumb to the weight of the snow. The place where it had been was immediately undetectable. Weighed down by our heavy rucksacks and breaking through the crust of black ice, we returned to the lower camp. The snowstorm had started up again and the wind whipped fragments of frozen black snow from under our feet and into our faces, making breathing difficult. We stopped for a rest on a high ridge. The gigantic cone of the volcano was revealed from its summit to its foundations. Fountains of lava rhythmically showered the cinder cone and the sounds of the explosions reached us a fraction of a second later. A black, forked river filled the valley, disappearing below, at the edge of the forest. Along the sides were black and white hieroglyphs – the work of storm-force winds, ash and snow. The air shook. A cloud of ash rose above the cinder cone. With a roar like a receding storm, Klyuchevsky was engulfed and a black mane of ash stretched over the surrounding hills.

We had not been prepared fully for this eruption. We did not have all the necessary cameras and equipment, transport or even radio communications. Only enthusiasm and persistence kept our expedition going in such inhuman conditions, collecting scientific data, finding patterns in stormy, and, at first glance, unpredictable phenomena. We had realized an ambition neatly expressed in the traditional farewell exchanged between vulcanologists: 'I hope you are caught in a catastrophic eruption'.

65

Left
Mount Klyuchevsky

Overleaf
Ostry and Plosky Tolbachik. In the distance are Bezymyannyy, Klyuchevsky and Plosky. Tolbachik is seen here and on the following spread as it appeared before the eruption of 1975.

Following spread
The Tolbachik plateau. The great Tolbachik explosion happened here, along the line of the fault-fissure.

The Tolbachik Eruption

Nine years after the Klyuchevsky eruption, seismology stations set up to monitor the Klyuchevsky group of volcanoes registered a spate of earthquakes emanating from the vicinity of Mount Tolbachik. This was the signal for an eruption. Ash rose one-and-a-half kilometres above Tolbachik; by night it reflected red from the volcano's molten core.

The time and place of the eruption were estimated from seismic data, field seismostations were set up, and a team of vulcanologists went out to the volcano. Events developed swiftly. On 6 July 1975, fourteen kilometres from the foot of the volcano, a fissure appeared along a broad lava plateau nine hundred metres above sea level. Above it swirled steam and gases, and it began to spit red-hot cinders. Over the next twenty-four hours lava spurted from the fissure, from a single mighty vent. The archetypal volcanic formation, the cinder cone, started to take shape. The wind carried the cloud of gases, ash and cinders to the south-east, leaving a trail of debris along its path.

The lava plateau known as the Tolbachik Valley is split by a deep fissure which stretches for sixty kilometres. The ancient but still active volcano of Tolbachik stands halfway across this crack. A new phase of basaltic volcanic activity started between ten and twenty thousand years ago when the fissure was first formed. Eruptions have occurred once every thirty years and some have lasted for many months, or even years. Vulcanologists have estimated the depth of the magma reservoir at between sixty and seventy kilometres beneath the earth's surface. The magma feeding into the reservoir rises from even greater depths. The eruptions that we witnessed were on level ground – there was no need to dig into the snow to set camp, or to cross ice-covered slopes.

Camp was established one-and-three-quarter kilometres from the site of the eruption. Nearby were fresh water, dwarf Siberian pine, bilberries and red whortleberries. The wind carried the ash to one side, away from us. Because access to the site was easy, tourists began to arrive. On one occasion, a woman even clambered out of a helicopter carrying a small baby.

Meanwhile, the strength of the eruption was still increasing rapidly. The magma, under extremely high pressure, was forced up the fault to the surface. The gases dissolved in the magma expanded with the force of an explosion. Scorching molten rocks spurted out in the stream of gases escaping from the fissure. Columns of rock splintered and crashed, and steam and gas shot up to a height of eleven kilometres. During the day it was dark and evil, with glowing fragments. At night it glowed with all the hues of molten metal.

Left
In the first stages of the eruption there was an enormous emission of gas from the magma, rising up by way of an underground water channel. As the expanding gases reached the surface their force threw up red-hot rocks, cinders, ash and steam, forming the classic volcanic structure – the cinder cone.

Overleaf
A column of splintered rock, gases and ash, rising to a height of twelve kilometres.

Then the wind changed unexpectedly and the ash cloud turned towards the camp. Rain mixed with ash and large cinders and stones fell on the tents. A layer of cinders seventy centimetres thick fell on the camp in a single night. Practically all the equipment and seismostations were put out of action, buried under layers of cinders. The roar of the volcano mingled with the rolls of thunder. In the middle of the day it was almost completely dark, except when the curtain of flying stones was illuminated by flashes of lightning. All plant life disappeared, the tattered tents sagged under the increasing weight of cinders, and our water source was smothered.

We set up a new camp further from the volcano, in a depression surrounded by ridges of hardened lava – tents with frames were erected and an awning put up over the camp-fire to protect it from rain and falling cinders. It was warm and quiet. Mosquitoes still buzzed around. Between the volcano and the camp lay a dense forest, and nearby, through the silver birches and shrubs, was a deep, clear lake. Four kilometres away, but framed in the landscape in front of us, was the erupting volcano. In front of us the full grandeur of the eruption was played out with an overwhelming beauty and dynamism. At first we enjoyed it, but eventually tiredness caught up with us and we went to sleep.

Geodesists were at work at the northern foot of the mountain. Beneath layers of lava, in deep caves, they found the perfect protection for themselves and their instruments, with its own source of meltwater. It needed a special courage for them to shut themselves up in a stone trap in immediate proximity to the erupting volcano. It later transpired that they had been directly above the fault line and the ensuing eruption happened right beneath them. More than once 'bombs' of hot rock flew in through the entrance, smashing the protective wooden doors.

The grey of dusk subsided into the black of night. A purple glow illuminated the swirl of flying cinders from within, made all the brighter by flashes of lightning. The denser the disintegrated matter, the more frequent the discharges. Sometimes they were at intervals of only a few seconds, hampering radio communications and interfering with the accuracy of the instruments. At midnight a strange light appeared above the cone – a brown-green moon was glowing between the black clouds.

As we were trying to predict what might happen next, a new fissure opened up on the slope of the neighbouring peak, abutting onto the foot of the volcano – magma broke through the surface at a weak point and soon one edge had risen by forty metres, exposing layers of volcanic rock. The eruption now entered a new phase: there were not only explosions caused by expanding gases, but also effusions of already partially degassed molten lava.

Right and overleaf
The Tolbachik eruption.

At first the lava flowed in thin, separate lines. Then these joined in a stream which was both wider and faster, moving at three hundred metres per hour. The front of the stream glowed a bright crimson even in sunlight. Soon it reached the outskirts of the forest and gases mixed with smoke from the burning wood. The helicopter landing area and the water supply were already under threat. The undulating line of flames stretched across four kilometres. Everyone feared for the lake. Within two hours the lava stream was running by the water's edge. The trees by the lake caught fire and the lava flow teetered on the brink. Red chunks broke off and crashed into the water with muffled roars. Steam shrouded the trees – a white cloud veered to one side, broke away, and the lake suddenly ceased to exist. Together with the helicopter pad, it disappeared beneath the lava.

Although the camp was out of danger, we were now in another world. The trees, mosquitos, birds and blue sky were all gone. A blue haze hovered over the red-hot moving flow of lava. Previously the lava had been above us, and we had gone further downhill. Now the flow was far down the valley, getting broader, even climbing the valley walls, and we were safely to one side of it. Behind us was a hilly desert of cinders and dead trees, still and colourless. Crows circled above it on the lookout for other birds and small animals killed by the fallout. It was impossible to see where the lake and the helicopter landing pad had been. On the horizon the countryside was covered with a mist which made everything seem one-dimensional. Only one colour existed here - grey. It blended with the clouds, the sky, the weather and the landscape, but in such a complex variety of shades that it could never be dull.

At 4pm on 1 August the northern breach opened up. Lava broke through at the foot of the cone. Blue smoke, followed immediately by a fountain of lava, signalled the birth of a new lava flow. The bright, molten stream flowed ceaselessly, sometimes spraying over two hundred metres at an angle of forty-five degrees. The lava spread over the earlier flows and by evening had reached the camp. At midnight the guard sounded the alarm. A part of the flow near the camp, previously immobile, had started to move. The nocturnal migration was like the biblical flight into Egypt: by the light of the volcano, our figures threw long, dark shadows, and out of the gloom of the night loomed the whitened skeletons of bushes. The weather was worsening; the noise of the wind and the distant roar of the volcano rounded off a foul night. Cinders and rain once more coated the tents and the tarpaulin. In such dangerous circumstances we slept with our clothes on.

79

The eruption continued with increased force at night, often accompanied by flashes of lightning and cracks of thunder.

Above
The lava flow incinerating the trees and plants in its path. A freshwater reservoir was destroyed in a matter of seconds.

Overleaf
The front of the lava flow stretched for several kilometres.

We were living in a changing and dangerous world. In the distance, the lead-grey, vertical spiral of flying rocks broadened out, and at the summit turned into a brightly coloured, unearthly cloud. The ground was ash grey, rough to the touch, resonant to the ear and completely devoid of water. It was difficult to imagine water on that porous surface. The few surviving creatures quivered helplessly - broken birds, mice, bears in search of water, and wood grouse. But there was no dust. Whatever the column of ash carried upwards, now only porous stones rained down on our heads.

The cinders levelled out the hills, and the hollows filled up. Walking was easy. Below us was the ruined forest. Beneath the tarpaulin the fire was kept constantly alight. There was plenty of firewood, and whenever it rained we collected the water running off the tarpaulin in bowls and buckets. Filtered through cinders, the water tasted brackish and bitter. Once, we added a spoonful of soda to a particularly bitter bowl, and the reaction was immediate, an explosion like a small geyser. The tea smelled like stewed fruit and tasted disgusting. There was also no escape from the wind, which blew cold and silent, plastering our clothes, faces and cameras with rain and mud. The eruption was now at its peak and the cone was deformed. Explosions in a channel destroyed the walls, throwing up chunks of deep-lying sedimentary rocks - snow-white sandstone and limestone, painted with black volcanic matter. We came across stones still covered with plant life. Fountains of lava pulsed, throwing up fragments and flowing like water down the steep slopes, splashing and making waves. After a month of this frantic activity, everything went quiet. The crater was silent, the lava still. By this time, the cinder cone had reached a height of three hundred metres. However, puzzlingly, the seismographs were once more registering volcanic activity. A group of vulcanologists went in search of a few last pieces of lava. They sat down to smoke a cigarette. Suddenly, a black fissure zigzagged across in front of them. Gases and steam rose and fountains of fine lava shot up. The fissure was widening before their eyes. They tried to measure the speed at which the walls were moving apart, and jumped from one side to the other to see what was hidden deep underground. They had witnessed the birth of a second volcano. By the following day, fountains of lava were reaching eight hundred metres.

In the middle of August, after a short silence, to the north of the new cone a third volcano erupted with a roar and a fountain of blue lava. The eruption was intense and the third cone developed very fast.

At the end of August the eruption concentrated on the second cone. The other cones went quiet.

85

Far from the centre of the eruption, and untouched by the lava flow, trees and plants were killed by the weight of the cinder fall.

Some years after the eruption the
area around the volcano still looks
like a wasteland

87

Only the tops of skeleton trees can
be seen, their trunks buried in
the cinders.

88

The bleak landscape, buried deep
under ash and ominously quiet after
the eruption.

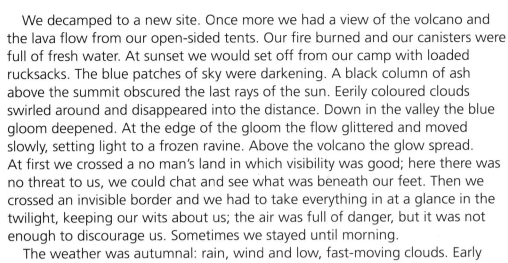

We decamped to a new site. Once more we had a view of the volcano and the lava flow from our open-sided tents. Our fire burned and our canisters were full of fresh water. At sunset we would set off from our camp with loaded rucksacks. The blue patches of sky were darkening. A black column of ash above the summit obscured the last rays of the sun. Eerily coloured clouds swirled around and disappeared into the distance. Down in the valley the blue gloom deepened. At the edge of the gloom the flow glittered and moved slowly, setting light to a frozen ravine. Above the volcano the glow spread. At first we crossed a no man's land in which visibility was good; here there was no threat to us, we could chat and see what was beneath our feet. Then we crossed an invisible border and we had to take everything in at a glance in the twilight, keeping our wits about us; the air was full of danger, but it was not enough to discourage us. Sometimes we stayed until morning.

The weather was autumnal: rain, wind and low, fast-moving clouds. Early September brought nothing remarkable - the colours of autumn did not appear anywhere on the grey desert. Snow fell on the mountains. The new cones were still black and active. We shivered in the cold wind, sitting alongside a heat of above a thousand degrees, sometimes warming and drying ouselves near the lava flow. The dank wind had wiped away any lingering signs of summer.

91

One morning in the middle of September we were woken with a jolt by the absolute silence. It was highly unusual - the unending background noise had disappeared. Even the weather was quiet. Barely noticeable wisps were rising above the crater, lit from beneath by a rosy glow. The eruption was over. Three truncated hills stood in a deserted landscape. In parts they were shadowed a violet-black from the clouds hovering over them, in parts a yellow-brown from the rays of the low autumnal sun. Between them lay new expanses of cinders.

During the day we walked to the base of the cones. The huge, round rocks appeared even larger close up. They were covered in skins of lava – coated in it, like heads of cabbage. They had been thrown up or poured out from the heart of the volcano by the more powerful explosions, and had then rolled down the inner side of the cone, picking up lumps of viscous lava. Our impression was that of a giants' battlefield, quiet, dead and motionless. After the week of ceaseless noise, the fresh air and the silence were almost as striking as the eruption itself.

The eruption is over. Secondary fires caused by oxidizing processes are burning on the many cinder cones. Complex chemical compounds and mineral deposits are in the process of forming. The colourful results of sublimation can be seen on the upper slopes of the cinder cones even from a distance. The oxidization and the resultant fires will continue for many years.

Another day passed quietly. Low cloud hid everything around us and fog surrounded our tent. After such upheaval the quiet seemed ominous. Radios bridged the gap between the different camps with an endless stream of questions - what had happened, and where? That evening the seismologists warned us to monitor the lava vent of the southernmost of the three cones. There would be an eruption at midday. During the day cumulus clouds appeared high in the sky behind the cones with a strange coloration - the colour one finds with gas and dust. Then far down the valley we saw blue smoke above the lava vent. The eruption was continuing. We named the first group of cones formed in the Tolbachik Valley the Northern Breach. This new eruption we would call the Southern Breach.

This eruption was different from the northern one. The chemical make-up of the lava and gases had changed. There were few pyroclasts - the violent eruptions of fiery, disintegrated matter. Instead, there was a gentle outpouring of molten lava. As it moved, new channels piled up on the cooling flows. Rivers of lava ran along tunnels under the hardened crust, forming lava lakes. Whenever we had a spare moment we collected souvenirs from amongst the molten lava – crystals of feldspar, which fell in abundance with the cinders, in clusters or in the form of circular plates.

There was volcanic activity on Plosky Tolbachik at the time of the eruptions of the Southern and Northern Breaches. Above its crater swirled an ash cloud, sometimes reaching a height of two kilometres. It formed a link between the eruptions in the valley and the volcano itself. The volcano Plosky Tolbachik forms a single massif with the older volcano, Ostry Tolbachik. Plosky Tolbachik has a flat summit, more than four kilometres in diameter. This saucer-shaped caldera is a result of settlement at the summit after earlier outpourings of lava from the fissures in Tolbachik Valley. Within the larger outer caldera is a smaller one about one-and-a-half kilometres in diameter, in which there is an active crater – a well 150 metres deep and 300 metres across. From the edge of the crater splashes of molten lava and red hot rocks are visible in the interior. In 1970, a lava lake formed at the bottom of the well, and could clearly be seen from the air. This activity increased the diameter and depth of the crater. At the same time a mass of ice melted and formed a hot lake in the well. By the time the 1975 eruption finally finished in December 1976, the lava flows had changed the geography of the entire area.

We had witnessed the largest recorded basalt eruption in the Kurilo-Kamchatka region. Research into the material that was collected will take many years and should fill an important place in the study of the geology of the planet.

The results of sublimation forming
unusual mineral shapes.

Mounts Gorely and Mutnovsky

These volcanoes form part of the southern volcanic range of Kamchatka, and are separated from the eastern range by a depression which cuts the peninsula from west to east along the latitude of Avacha Bay. They were the result of ancient volcanic activity which formed basaltic volcanoes. The peaks of these were destroyed by huge explosions which formed vast, deep calderas. Volcanic formations from later eruptions have grown up on the slopes of these early shield volcanoes. The volcanoes Mutnovsky and Gorely and their near neighbours, close to Petropavlovsk, Koryak and Avacha, were formed in this way. Their cones are formed from andesite lava or cinders from eruptions. These volcanoes are an intrinsic part of the modern Kamchatka skyline. Some are constantly active, others are quiet or have sporadic fumarole activity, as in the cases of the Uzon Caldera, on the slopes of Kikhpinich, and on Kosheleva.

Mutnovsky, 2,324 metres high, is one of the most active volcanoes in Kamchatka. The caldera is somewhat irregular in shape, with a diameter of ten kilometres at the widest part, formed from two cones, destroyed and mutilated by eruptions. Nowadays, volcanic activity is concentrated in the northern part of the caldera. Here, glaciers lie between rocky massifs which have been shaped by exposure to constant high temperatures and acidic solutions. In the crater left by an explosion at the western ridge of the volcano, the red glow of hot lava is sometimes visible. In many places in the caldera there are columns of sulphurous gases, and hot lakes, cauldrons and fumaroles throwing out droplets of hot sulphur.

Left
Inside the crater of Mount Mutnovsky. Mutnovsky is a complex, multi-cratered volcano, one of the most active in Kamchatka.

Overleaf
The centre of the volcano is pitted with funnels and cauldrons of boiling mud, with yellow and black mounds and columns of sulphur and highly acidic streams. Above this hovers a cloud of toxic gases.

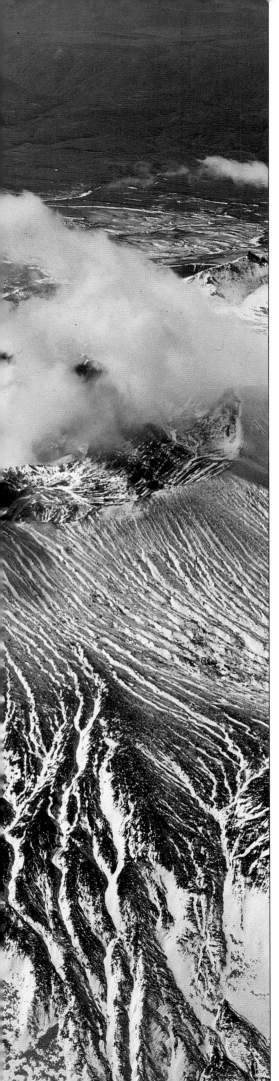

Mutnovsky's nearest neighbour is Gorely. Although not so high, it has a massive base and a volcanic spinal ridge covered by craters, forming an elliptical caldera between nine and fourteen kilometres wide. Several craters are active periodically. From time to time lakes form at the bottom of these, heated by eruptions. The walls of the craters are steep, revealing layers of porous deposits, laid down during the volcano's many eruptions. On a clear day, grey columns of cloud or cumulus formations accompanied by clouds of ash are visible from Petropavlovsk. There are cinder cones and expanses of cooled lava on the slopes of both the caldera and the volcano itself.

99

Left
Mount Gorely. An active volcano with many craters. Several of these are periodically active, throwing out gases, clouds of ash and jets of steam. The walls of the craters are steep, with layers of porous deposits providing evidence of previous eruptions. From time to time small lakes form in the craters, warmed by the hot rock below.

Overleaf
Mount Gorely is constantly active to a greater or lesser extent. One of its sporadic eruptions of gas, steam and ash is shown here.

Following spread
The River Mutnaya flows out of the crater. The highly acidic water cuts through the walls of the crater and the deep glacier. The acids are formed in the many hot lakes, cauldrons of boiling mud, and fumaroles. The River Mutnaya is so acidic that no fish can live in it, even at the point where it enters the Pacific.

Sulphur deposited by sulphurous
gases forced up from deep within the
volcano.

The northern face of the volcano is split by a tectonic fault. The River Mutnaya plunges over one hundred metres into the fissure. In the walls of the canyon are layers of lava from ancient eruptions.

The Kronotsky Nature Reserve

The Kronotsky Nature Reserve was established to protect the natural environment created by volcanic activity both past and present. It is representative of the whole of Kamchatka, encompassing some unique natural features. The park forms part of a worldwide system of reserves protected in order to preserve the biosphere, and its unique natural and geophysical features rank it amongst the most important in the world. It is one of the largest in Russia, covering more than a million hectares.

The reserve contains the majority of the volcanoes of the eastern volcanic chain on Kamchatka. The north-east boundary of the reserve is ringed by the mountainous massif of the Kronotsky peninsula with its steep, rocky slopes and the largest ice field in Kamchatka. Ice covers more than eleven thousand hectares of the peninsula. Most of the volcanoes within the reserve are extinct, their activity limited to high-temperature jets of steam and gases, and the constant presence of hot springs and geysers. These same processes also created the Valley of Geysers and the Uzon Caldera, described and discussed in Chapters 7 and 8, and the fumarole field of Burlyashchy Volcano, with its multi-coloured fields of vein minerals, and cauldrons full of black, boiling mud. The thermal springs are colonized by brightly coloured bacteria and algae.

The eastern border of the reserve runs along more than three hundred kilometres of Pacific coastline. There is a rich variety of coastal landscapes: bays, lagoons, sandy shallows, reefs and precipices. The cliffs are home to bird colonies, and the sea washes up debris which attracts scavenging birds and animals. Bears often wander along the shore or swim in the sea. They search for berries in the tundra which runs down to the ocean in a narrow belt.

The ocean affects the climate of the coastal region: the sharp winter frosts, common elsewhere in Kamchatka, are absent here, snowfalls are heavy, damp clouds frequent. Hurricanes are born and pick up speed over the ocean before hitting the coast, hence the strong, stunted forms of the trees along the coast - rowan, dwarf silver birch and Siberian pine, willow and alder. Forests of stone birch bend in the direction of the prevailing wind. In sheltered ravines are thick-trunked trees with dense undergrowth and tall grasses.

Left and overleaf
Mount Kronotsky. One of the most beautiful volcanoes in Kamchatka, with a perfectly formed cone cut by ribs and barrancas. At its foot lies Lake Kronotskoye, overleaf, the largest on the peninsula. The lake is fed from underground. Lava flows originally cut off the channel of the river. Salmon were trapped in the lake, and some species died, unable to adapt to the change from their nomadic life. However, the red salmon adjusted to spawning in the shallow parts of the lake and the tiny streams that still flow into it.

My own first visit to the reserve was made in 1964. There were three of us, travelling with a local guide, pack horses and a dog. Our journey started in a small fishing village on the shores of the ocean. The path led along the top of a steep cliff. Below us the waves of the Pacific washed a wide beach. The ocean was grey, the sky leaden. Seagulls were everywhere. Ahead of us lay complete isolation; the nearest settlement was more than sixty kilometres away.

Turning inland, a small river crossed the path. Two logs spanned it. We stopped in the middle and in the fast-flowing current we could see a large shoal of huge loach and salmon. Next, we came to an estuary. A narrow, gently curving spit divided a large reservoir from the ocean. This formation occurs frequently here: rivers wash down sedimentary rock, and the ocean washes it straight back again. The river heaps up sand-bars shielded by the steep ocean shoreline. Low clouds rose above the estuary like a blue forest along the horizon. The perfectly symmetrical cone of Kronotsky volcano emerged out of the mist. We crossed into the reserve at its southernmost tip. We planned to walk along its southern border, to follow the banks of the River Stary Semlyachik to the foot of the volcano Maly Semlyachik, and then to travel north to the Uzon Caldera. We had chosen this route because it was completely deserted. At first the path was clearly marked, but soon it disappeared altogether.

We had not even gone a kilometre when a wild mare and her two foals started to follow us, sometimes closely behind us, sometimes at a distance to one side. The path climbed. Somewhere nearby we could hear a river. From time to time we crossed patches of cinders, evidence of old volcanic activity. There were mushrooms everywhere - brown, boletus and orange cap. Whoever was in charge of the horses had a hard time of it. On level ground there was no need to hurry after them, but once on a slope they quickened their pace, leaving their minder gasping for breath.

Right
Mount Krashennikov. Lying to the south of Lake Kronotskoye, it is 1,859 metres high and has two cones and two craters at the summit, forming a ridge. The volcano rises above a caldera nine kilometres in diameter. During the spring thaw the snowdrifts often form bizarre shapes.

Overleaf
The volcanoes of the Gamchensk group form part of the eastern volcanic range of Kamchatka and display a wide variety of volcanic features, among them cinder cones, lava flows, fumarole fields and crater lakes.

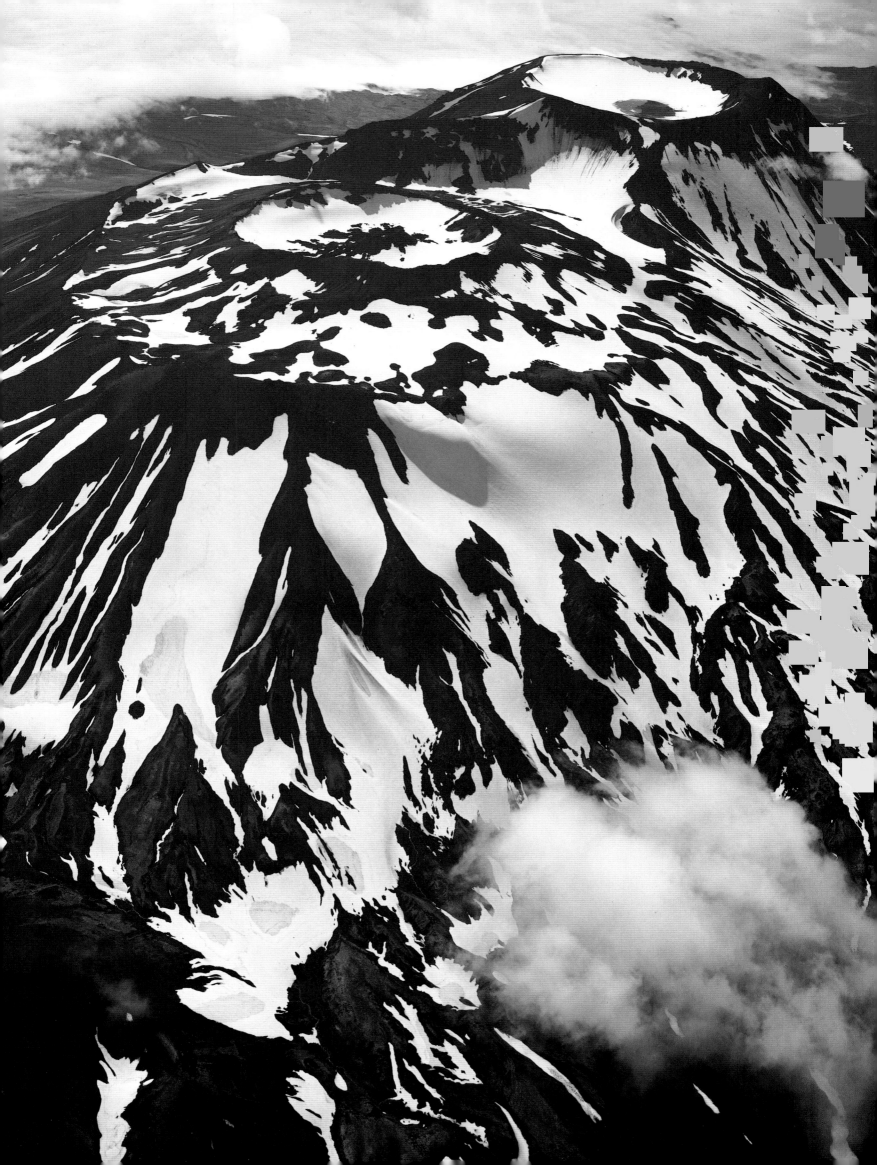

At last we emerged from the woods and the countryside opened out. A hard day closed with a cold, bright evening. Free of their packs, the horses galloped around, the foals pacing amongst the pack, poking their noses into everything. We put up the tents and lit the camp fire. It projected a warm circle into the limitless night, illuminating the retreating trees. The dawn was milky white. Wisps of mist hovered above the river, clinging to the trunks of the trees. It was damp and cold. The only warm air was above the camp fire, where a blue smoke curled upwards.

A sunny morning developed to reveal a wonderful landscape - volcanoes, valleys and thickets of trees. At first there was no need for maps or compasses, but a wall of grey cloud was moving off from the ocean, and the countryside was gradually obscured. It became damp and cold, and visibility was cut to only a few metres. The track soon disappeared and rain began to fall. Rain in Kamchatka is not like rain in Central Russia. The air becomes saturated with tiny drops. Water poured off the grass and bushes at the slightest touch. Horses and people a few metres ahead were lost in an incorporeal gloom. The thickets of dwarf Siberian pine and alder were impenetrable. The only option was to navigate around them. Sometimes the thickets suddenly fell away, and the whole caravan found itself sliding down a steep, overgrown slope. At the bottom of these gullies was often a flat, dried-up water channel. Occasionally it would run in the direction in which we were headed. Such gullies were numerous - steep-sided and deep, with the marks of water erosion. In some places water trickled down from snowdrifts and after a few metres disappeared into porous cinders. Elsewhere water percolated through to great depths to form fast-flowing underground rivers, which emerged through the rock face in the form of waterfalls.

We managed to see much on that trip, as the photographs in this chapter testify. We visited the fumarole fields on Burlyashchy, the Uzon Caldera and the Valley of Geysers. Then we returned to the Pacific coast where the ocean greeted us with a roar of surf - somewhere out there another storm was brewing.

A stone birch, one of the most widely distributed trees on Kamchatka.

116

View from the bank of Lake
Kronotskoye, the largest freshwater
lake on Kamchatka.

Dwarf or pygmy willow, lichens,
willowherb and various grasses,
the first plants to reappear on the
cinder fields.

Left
Every species of plant unique to
Kamchatka can be found in the
Kronotsky Nature Reserve. Most of
the land is covered by forests of
stone birch and a varied, dense
undergrowth.

Above
Brown bear foraging for berries on
the Kamchatkan tundra.

Overleaf
View out across the Pacific Ocean
from the shores of the reserve.

The Valley of Geysers

The Kamchatka geysers were discovered in the spring of 1941. A small group of geologists were researching the completely unstudied territory of the Kronotsky Nature Reserve. Tatyana Ustinova, now a doctor of geology and mineralogy, led the group. The route took them across a deep, barely accessible valley on the tectonic fault. A cursory glance at this secret ravine indicated nothing especially interesting. Vertical walls, with steeply falling scree in narrow gullies, disappeared into deep undergrowth, drained by little culverts. Alder, dwarf Siberian pine, spreading rowan and birch made even the flat plateau inaccessible. At this point the party became trapped. The further they descended into the valley, the clearer it became that it would be impossible to turn round and climb out. Only when evening fell, by which time they were soaked from head to foot, with badly torn clothing, did they reach a small, warm-water river. Opposite, down a narrow vertical crevice, plunged the River Shumnaya in full spate, flowing out of the caldera of the Uzon volcano.

Unexpectedly, from right beneath their feet arose a strange roar, and a jet of boiling water shot up at an oblique angle from the direction of the river. Shrouded in a white cloud this powerful fountain rose up, subsided into the river and, just as unexpectedly, disappeared. Nobody had any real understanding of geysers at that time. This, the first of Kamchatka's geysers to be discovered, was given the name *Pervenets* meaning 'First Born', and the unknown warm river, a tributary of the River Shumnaya, was named Geyzernaya. Since that date, the Valley of Geysers has been fully explored; now nobody would think of following the almost impassable route which led to its accidental discovery.

Left and overleaf
The reserve is home to a unique natural phenomenon – the Valley of Geysers, discovered in 1941. The valley displays a variety of thermal phenomena associated with gradually decreasing volcanic activity. In the central thermal field are several geysers, see overleaf. The different colours of the geyserites, left, are the result of the various microorganisms colonizing them, and of the heat and the mineral content of the water.

Detailed research of the valley was only started in 1945. The *Pervenets* geyser was located furthest downstream. Upstream, over a stretch of six kilometres, explorers found a great variety of thermal displays, associated with the subterranean heat of the Kikhpinich Volcano. Along both banks of the River Geyzernaya pours a concentration of hot, spouting, pulsing tributaries. The subterranean heat creates its own microclimate, so that even in April the glades are green, the first flowers are blooming, and early insects are beginning to appear. Many rare plants and grasses flourish there. Bears come here after their winter hibernation, some passing straight through, others lingering for several days. On my visits, sometimes there have been as many as twelve bears present at the same time. They have their own rules of association and females with newborn cubs avoid these big groups; a hungry male might forget his parental instincts. The young cubs, two or three years old, avoid the larger adults for the same reason. Cannibalism, especially in the first days after hibernation, is not unknown.

In May, Kamchatka is still under snow, but the thermal fields around the River Geyzernaya and the Uzon Volcano are already green. The fastest rivers, which are ice-free even in winter, grow wider and deeper. Small flocks of ducks and swans fly from place to place. There are no roads in the Kronotsky Nature Reserve, within which the Valley of Geysers is situated. Here and there are tracks worn by visitors. Access to the park is strictly limited and permission to carry out scientific experiments must be sought from the park administrators. Expeditions travel on horseback using guides with local knowledge. It is possible to bring groups in and out by helicopter, but air transport is restricted by long periods of weather unsuitable for flying. The usual approach to the Valley of Geysers lies from the Semyachinsky Estuary along the shore of the ocean. The route lies across several fast rivers. There are no bridges, and when the water level is high enough, fording the rivers can be fraught with dangers. All of these factors make access to the valley difficult.

126

The *Sakharniy*, or 'sugar' geyser, named for the geyserite around it, which is the colour of burnt sugar. It explodes sporadically with water at a temperature of 96 degrees centigrade.

The *Pervenets* ('First Born') geyser was
the first to be discovered by geologists
in 1941. In all there are twenty-five
large geysers in the valley.

Above
View down the centre of the Valley of the Geysers.

Overleaf left
A mud cauldron in the upper thermal field. With little water flowing in, the mud dries into distinctive shapes.

Overleaf right
Multicoloured thermophilic algae and bacteria living on geyserites.

The source of the River Geyzernaya is located at the foot of Kikhpinich. This volcano was last active some two hundred years ago, when the volcanic cone Savich was formed. Nowadays the area still carries much evidence of underground activity. Vents made by jets of gas are everywhere, the most common being carbonic acid and hydrogen sulphide gases. Green sulphides of arsenic are also found here. The colourful, hilly fields are crisscrossed by small streams, which form the source of the River Geyzernaya. In this region, which is even now rarely visited, scientists discovered in 1975 a small valley which became known as the Valley of Death. The area was a veritable cemetery of bears, foxes, rodents, crows and smaller birds. The animals had died in hollows, sheltered from the wind, and were found lying along the floors of deep trenches, in which poisonous gases had escaped. The greatest build-up of this natural pollution occurs in calm weather and can be dangerous even for humans. The location is certainly the most macabre of the many natural wonders to be found in the Valley of Geysers.

132

Right
The central and most active section of the valley, where several large geysers are grouped together.

Overleaf
The geyser named 'Malachite'. Typical of a pulsing spring, its unusual formation comes to an abrupt end in the warm water of the nearby River Geyzernaya.

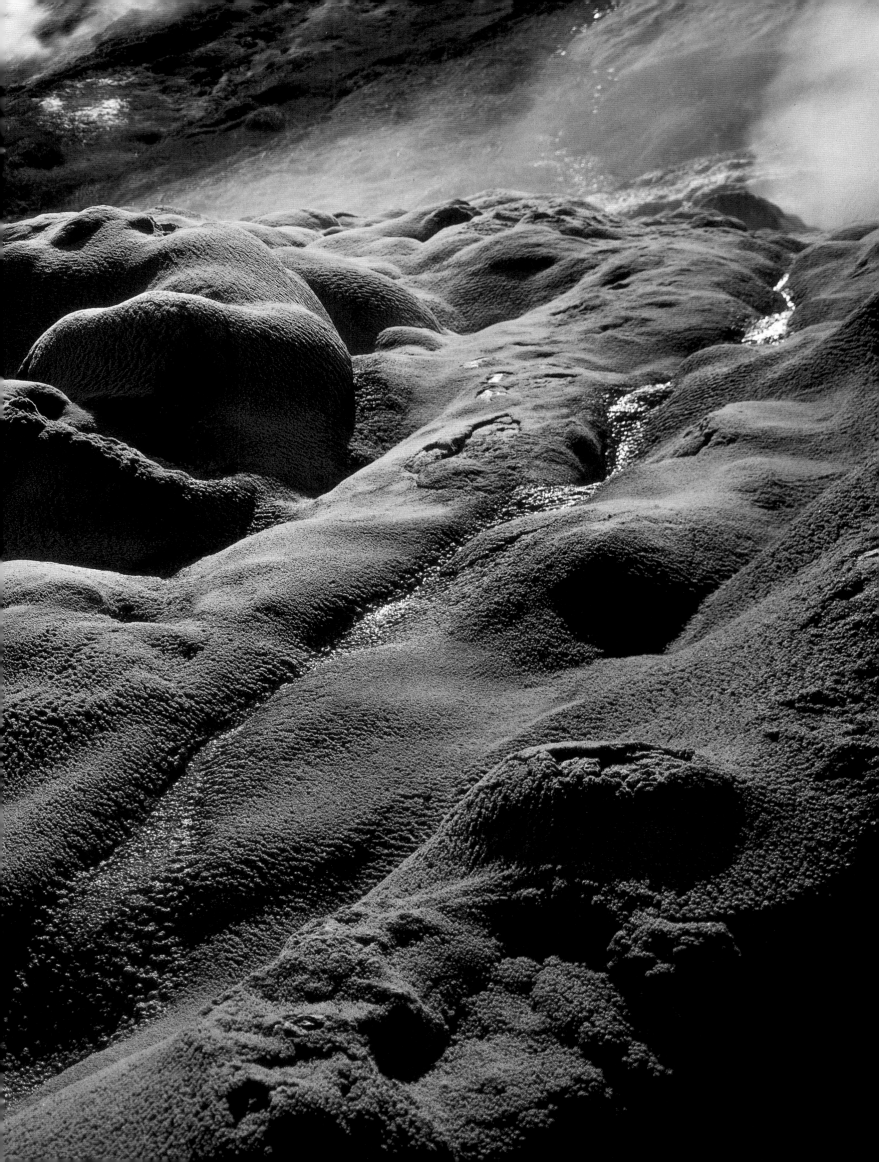

Above
The heavy frosts form ice formations
beside the geysers, which remain
unchanged until the spring thaw.

Right
Ancient, sedimentary volcanic rock
from the lake, exposed on the right
bank of the River Geyzernaya.

Left
Vodopadny Creek, a tributary of the
River Geyzernaya.

Above
Shoots of ramson, a species of wild
garlic, almost covered with snow.
Spring snowfalls and a return to the
freezing weather are common in
Kamchatka.

Overleaf and following spread
Winter and summer scenes in the
Uzon Caldera.

The Uzon Caldera

The Uzon Caldera is a ring structure which has undergone complex geological transformations during the hundreds of millennia of its existence. The crater was formed by the extraordinarily violent eruption of an earlier shield volcano, the crests of whose base can be made out on the caldera's western edge. Successive phases of lake formation have left layers of sedimentary rock. Prolonged periods of ice cover have also left their mark, and only in the last few millenia has the caldera assumed its present day appearance.

The flat bottom of the crater measures about fifteen kilometres by seven and a half, and is framed by great terraces between two hundred and nine hundred metres high. Its landscape consists of lakes, marshes, rivulets, and thermal areas above which steam rises incessantly from the numerous outlets of hot springs. The highest points of the caldera's surrounding ring are located on its western side: Mount Baranii, which rises to 1540 metres, and Mount Krasny which peaks 1320 metres above sea level. These are relics of the old active Mount Uzon volcano. The floor of the caldera slopes upwards to the north-east, and here, situated in a ring of pyroclastic rock at a height of between sixty and seventy metres is Lake Dalnyeye. A freshwater lake, it fills the crater left by a major eruption, is twenty-five metres deep in places, and has water of exceptional clarity. Although the lake has no outlets, there is a permanent fish population; the roe may have been introduced by birds carrying them from the River Shumnaya, three kilometres away.

On a visit to the caldera some years ago, my party followed the little-used path from another volcano, Maly Semyachik. The weather turned against us on the first day. A light, irksome rain was falling, and yet all trace of running water had been left somewhere behind us. We saw dry runnels in the porous slag, but we were soaked through. On the following morning, armed with saucepans, we collected water, shaking it off the bushes of bog whortleberry. We wandered among the ravines and over the tundra cloaked in an impenetrable fog and accompanied by fine, drizzling rain. Even when it stopped for a time, a mist of water droplets hung in the air and settled on everything. The people of Kamchatka call this atmospheric humidity *bus*, or beads. We pitched camp for the night and a blanket of fog rolled over in waves and the rain drummed on the pitched roof of the tent. We could barely keep the campfire alight, and the smoke circled from it in every direction. Water seeped through the tent seams, and soaked into everything from underneath.

145

Left and overleaf
The Uzon Caldera. A unique natural phenomenon, displaying the effects of the deep-seated heat of the magma reservoir.

Bad weather in Kamchatka is a grey gloom. Even the lowest mountains are cut off by the fog, and the magnificent landscape is completely hidden. It was in this kind of fog that we lost the horses. A great wet heap of packs, saddles, and our rucksacks lay forlornly in the wet tundra. It was too heavy for us to carry ourselves, and we couldn't leave it with any hope of ever finding it again. Our guide disappeared into the fog to look for the horses. Time passed, unhurried. Then, in complete silence a dog came bounding out of the fog, with the horses behind it, and our guide behind them on horseback.

On several occasions we saw bears and deer, and once our path was crossed by a family of arctic sheep. There were also many sightings of ptarmigan and hares. Although we seemed to be walking around in circles in the brushwood and the fog we eventually arrived on the rim of the caldera. The fog drew back like a theatre curtain, and our caravan was outlined in sharp silhouette against the backdrop of a threatening sky and blue-black walls mottled with snow pockets. The sight which was suddenly revealed was so strange that at first we could not believe our eyes.

We were dumbstruck by this lost world. Beneath a louring sky, distant swans were calling to each other, and in a haze of mist beneath the cloud loons shrilled. As if to authenticate the primeval quality of this foggy land, a bear lumbered across the emerald green of vast marshes that were crisscrossed by the floodwaters of the many lakes.

Right
Late morning mist clearing over the marshes.

Overleaf
Autumn on the Uzon Caldera.

Following spread
The Uzon Caldera has its own microclimate, resulting from the heated soil, hot springs and enclosed surroundings.

In early spring, when the ground is still covered in snow, bears that have wakened from hibernation make their way to the caldera. Sandpipers, ducks, and swans winter on the warm lakes, usually individually or in small flocks, but on our arrival, in late summer, all was a commotion of competing calls. Bear tracks were everywhere. We found their resting places, too, beside the mud cauldrons where they evidently warmed themselves. They are undeterred by the turbulent boiling waters and steam from the springs or, indeed, by the fumes of hydrogen sulphide. Bears are sagacious animals, and we followed their paths with confidence, even in places which seemed dangerous.

The caldera lives its own life, and enjoys its own microclimate. Even in winter, it retains oases of greenery. The warm air lifts the cloudbase above it, but the saucer is still misted by leaden thunderclouds at its edges.

Without taking our boots off - they were already sodden - we paddled through both the warm channels and the icy spring water. We decided to bivouac among the northern birches by a warm lake, and soon a plume of blue smoke was rising among the white columns of steam. Freed of their packs, the horses rolled and snorted in the grass. We sorted through our damp food and equipment, and pitched the tents.

That was my first visit to the caldera a few years ago. Although tourist visits are strictly limited, now there is a small log cabin in the caldera for those working in the reserve, modest, but centrally heated with thermal steam.

Right
A mud cauldron with characteristic dry mud formations.

Overleaf
Small glades of stone and silver birch trees are dotted about on the mud banks of the caldera.

158

Above and right
Bent and deformed stone birch,
typical of the Uzon Caldera. The
heavy snowfalls, many metres deep,
press the shrubs and trees down to
the ground, forcing them into
distorted shapes.

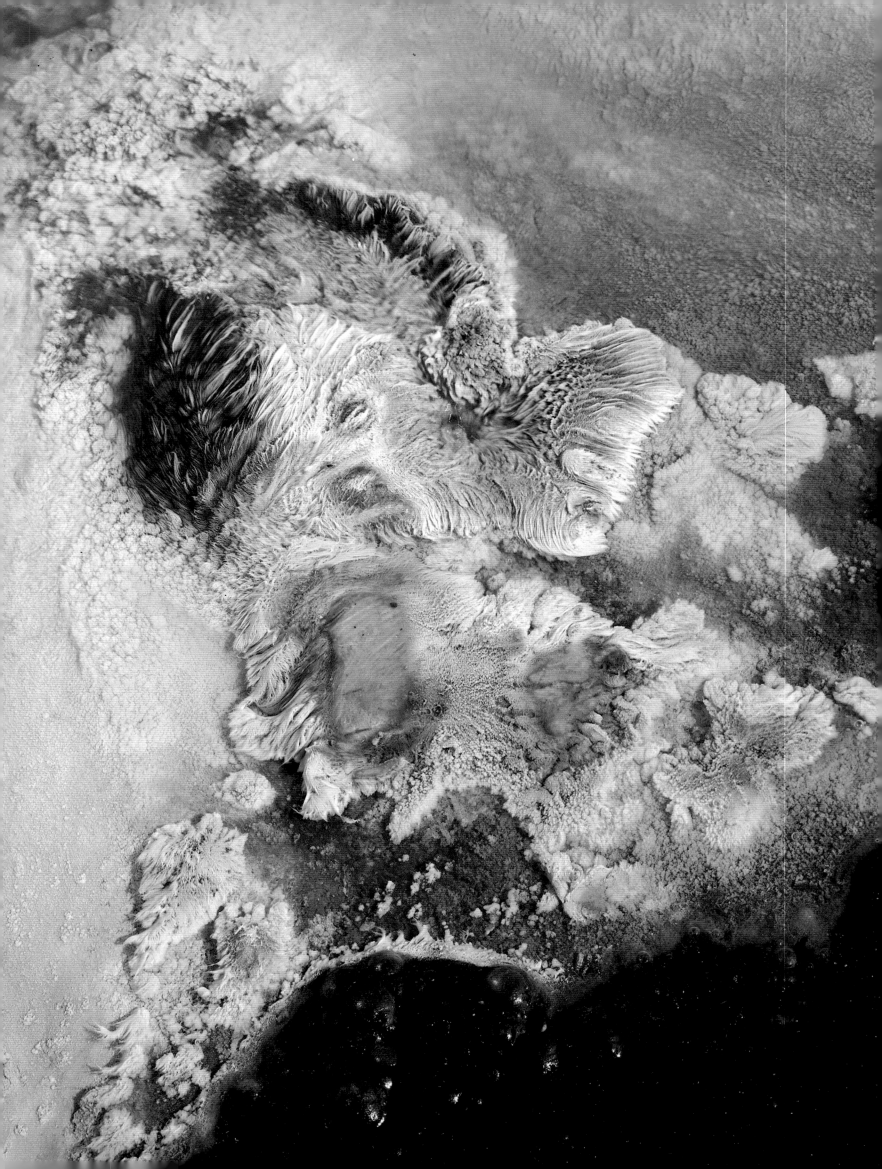

Cycles of volcanic activity can extend over millennia, a volcano remaining quiescent for many years before again becoming active. Ultimately eruptions cease, but in the depths of a volcano system, hearths of intensely hot magma can survive for thousands of years. They heat the rocks above them, and water seeping down is heated, becomes saturated with gases, and resurfaces. Seepage of surface water follows the tectonic cracks found in zones of volcanic activity.

Kamchatka possesses unique reserves of thermal water which vary in concentration and extent. The hot solutions emerging from far beneath the surface bring with them valuable information about the conditions under which mineral deposits are formed.

In the Uzon Caldera, boiling springs are concentrated in an area of sixty-one thousand square metres, in the form of lakes and springs, both large and small, with a high content of boron, silicon and ammonia, which are typically found in boiling solution. Fifteen sources of methylnaphthalene oil have also been found in the thermal areas.

The thermal areas have existed for many millennia. Their boiling springs are rich in minerals and have a variety of temperatures. With their steam and gases and the particular transformations they effect on rocks, they have caused the evolution of unique relations, combinations and developments of animal and vegetable life, which are to be found nowhere else in the world. These hearths of life are of interest to scientists from many fields. Their vulnerability in the natural environment of the present day demand from us an exceptional care and conservation.

161

Left and overleaf
Different varieties of algae live in springs of different temperatures. Blue-green algae survive in temperatures of up to sixty degrees centigrade while certain bacteria are accustomed to temperatures of up to ninety-six degrees. They form white columns around the thermal vents.

Following spread
The hot springs have the most varied concentrations and range of chemicals. Evaporation on the surface of the clay leaves compound crystals and colourful, amorphous deposits. Bubbles and foam filled with hydrogen sulphide float on the surface of the water, forming a film of sulphur.

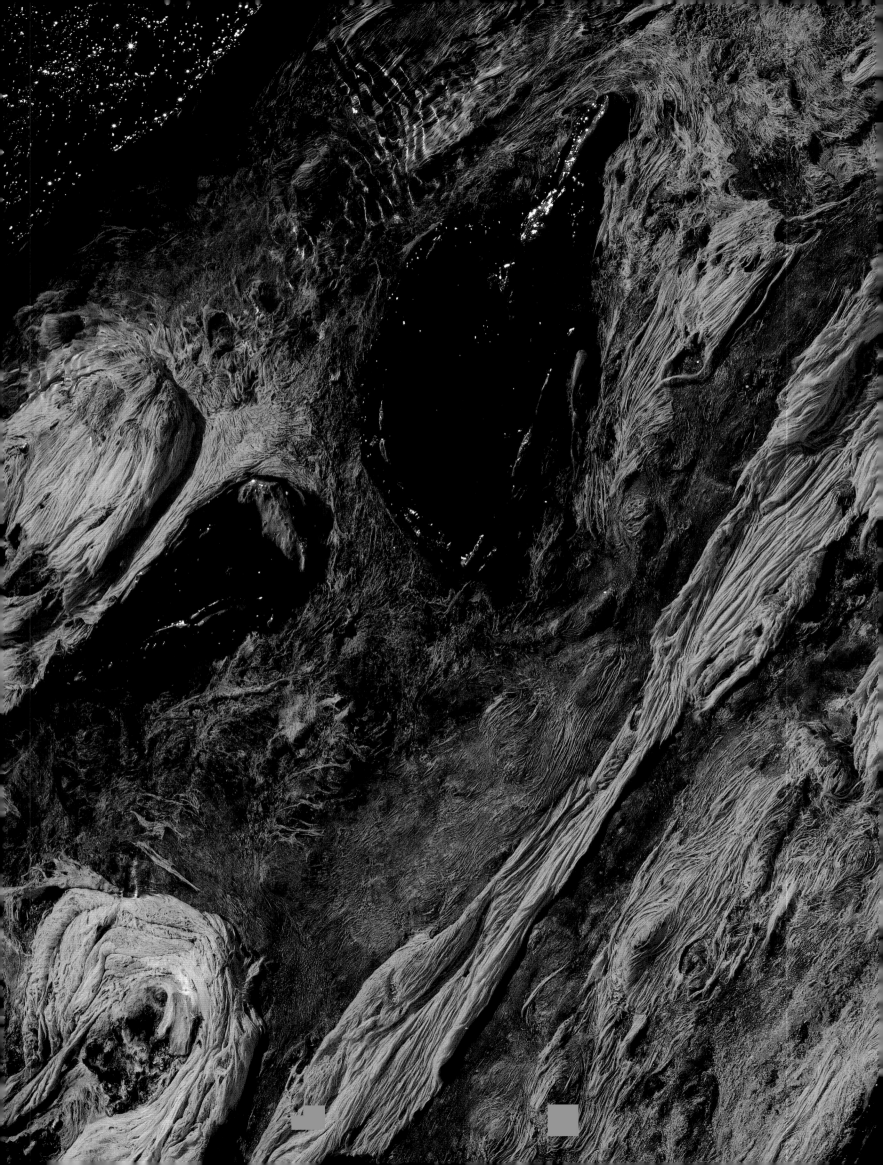

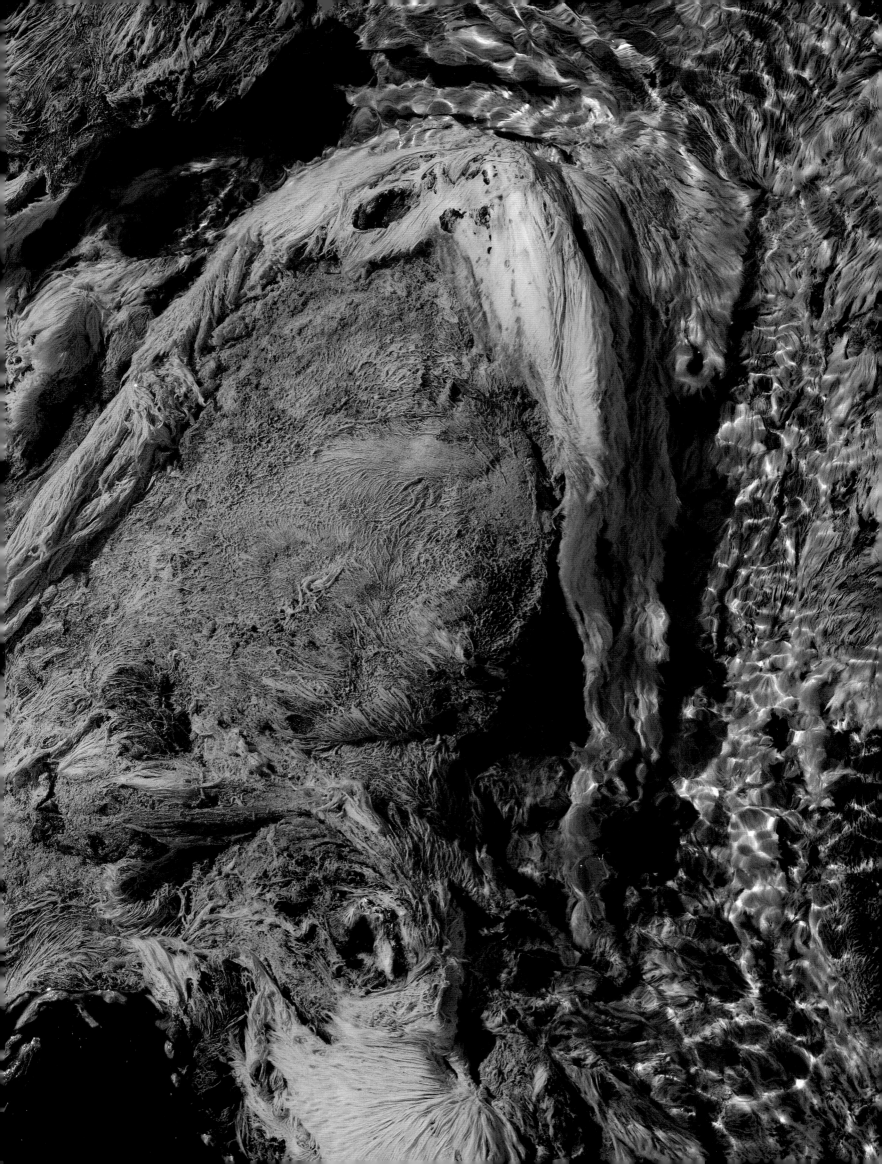

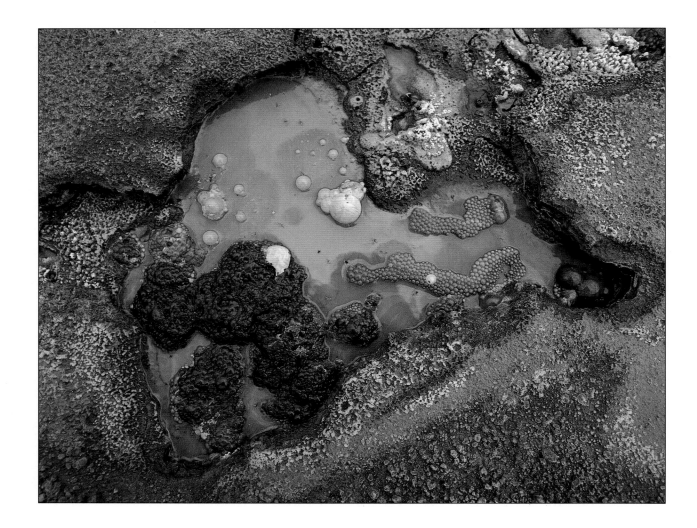

Above
Salts deposited on the surface of dried clay.

Right
A mud cauldron. Hot gas rises from deep underground, passing through rocks into fine clay, making wonderful, constantly changing patterns on the surface.

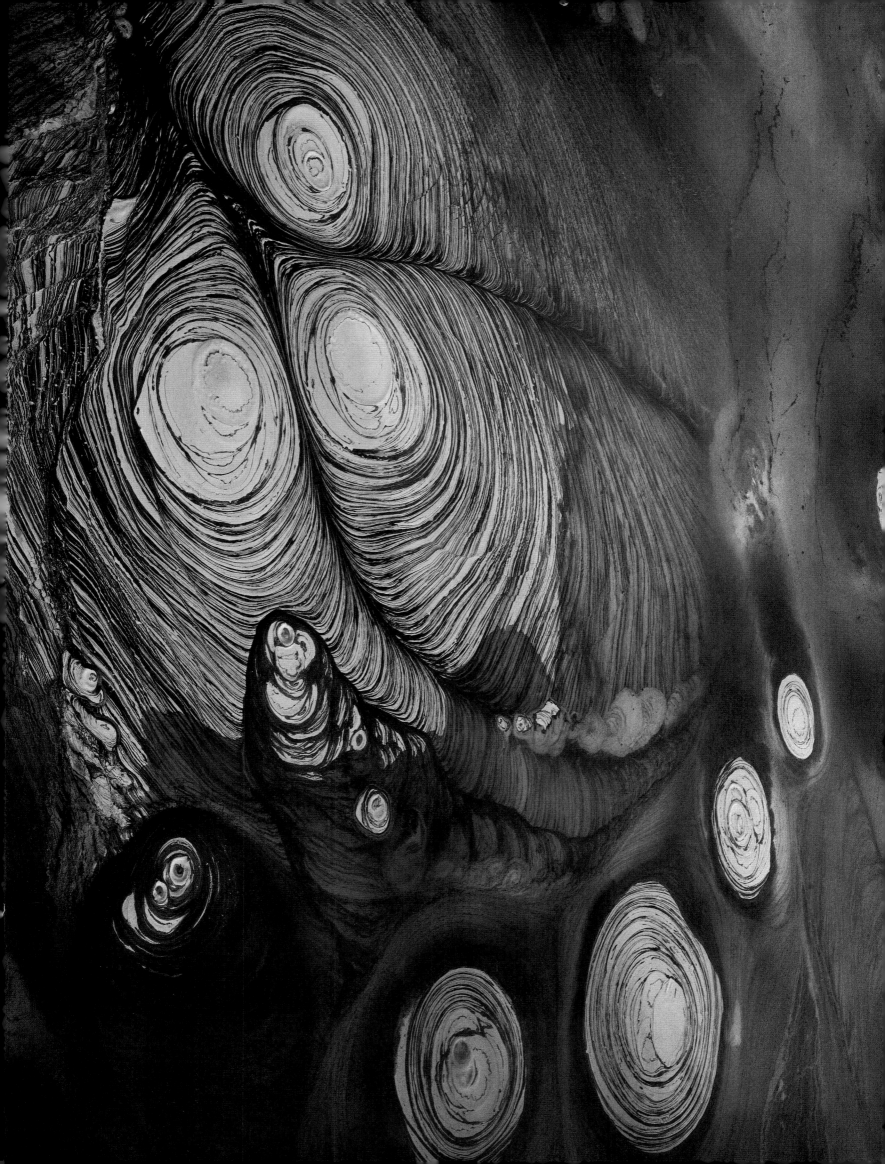

168

Above and right
Bears are widespread all over
Kamchatka and are constant visitors
to the Uzon Caldera. The abundance
of berries and edible plants also
attracts a variety of other animals and
birds, among them many partridges
and different species of sandpipers.
During the spring, migrating flocks of
ducks and swans rest there.

Overleaf
Autumn in the Uzon Caldera.

Left
The subterranean heat warms the outlying rocks. The surface waters percolate deep underground and absorb various chemicals and gases from the magma. On the surface they form an extraordinary system of hot lakes, springs and boiling cauldrons.

Above
Bear tracks appear everywhere, even on the surface of the hot clay.

174

Above and right
The flora of Kamchatka includes many
exotic species of lilies.

Overleaf
Looking east over the Pacific Ocean.

The Commander Islands

The people of Kamchatka once thought they saw land in the ocean to the east of the River Kamchatka estuary. In fact, what they saw was a dark mass of cloud hovering above the Commander Islands, one hundred and eighty-five kilometres away. The locals felt no need to make a dangerous journey of exploration. The Pacific Ocean is rarely peaceful, and the seaworthiness of their fishing vessels was not great. So the islands remained unexplored until the *St Peter,* a ship of the Second Kamchatka Expedition, landed there, where the crew suffered great hardships in the mistaken belief that they had reached Kamchatka.

On 29 May, 1741, two ships, the *St Peter* and the *St Paul,* set sail towards the coast of North America. The aim of the First Kamchatka Expedition had been discovery. The aim of the second was broader: to plot the whole northern sea passage, to explore Siberia from north to south, going as far east as possible. On the expedition were zoologists, botanists, geologists and ethnographers. One of its members was the famous German naturalist, Georg Wilhelm Steller. A second aim was the conquest of maritime lands and the establishment of economic and political links with other countries.

Bering had set off navigating by early charts on which Juan-de-Gama Land was marked. Under stormy conditions, the exhausted crew searched for this non-existent land, wasting valuable time and supplies. Finally convinced that the charts were inaccurate, both the *St Peter* and the *St Paul* headed for the Aleutian Islands, and from there eastwards. Losing each other in the storms, they reached the coast of America separately in July 1741.

The return journey was a tragic one. The *St Peter,* badly damaged, was barely steerable. One member of the expedition, Sven Vahsel, wrote in his diary 'Our boat drifted, like a piece of dead wood, practically without any steering, at the mercy of the waves and the wind, wherever they decided to send us.' On 4 November, the sailors sighted a high, unknown coastline and took it to be Kamchatka. They tried to drop anchor, but the high waves and the wind snapped the rotten ropes. The boat somehow passed through the offshore reef and into quieter waters.

It was only with great difficulty that the exhausted crew, suffering from scurvy, managed to land on the exposed shoreline, bringing off their dead and barely living companions with them. On this seemingly deserted island they buried twenty-eight seamen. On 8 December, Vitus Bering died. The island on which he ended his travels bears his name. The remaining crew wintered on the island, and then built a small craft from the wreckage of the first boat.

Mednnyy Island. The rock peaks are all that remain of volcanic foundations worn down by wind and water over thousands of years.

180

The Commander Islands. The dramatic
outline is formed by the remnants
of ancient volcanoes destroyed by
the ocean.

They finally reached the coast of Kamchatka in August 1742. The tragedy effectively put an end to the Second Kamchatka Expedition, and it was officially terminated on 20 September 1742. Despite all the hardships they endured, the members of the Kamchatka expeditions described and plotted the entire northern coastline of Russia and the basins of all the great Siberian rivers and lakes, made a topographical survey of the whole eastern coastline from the Chukotsk Peninsula to the mouth of the Amur, explored the Kurile and Aleutian Islands, and reached the shores of Alaska and Japan. The scientific research of the botanists, zoologists and ethnographers has lost none of its significance today.

The Commander Islands form a small archipelago, comprising two larger - Mednyy and Bering - islands and several much smaller ones. They were formed as a result of underwater eruptions and a subsequent rise in the sea floor in the region of a tectonic fracture. Evidence of their volcanic origins lies in the spherical or 'pillow' lava. On Mednyy Island there are two significant lava outflows beneath the surface of the ocean, located on Gladkov and Zhirov Bays. Layers of rock from later eruptions make up the crust of the island and can be seen in exposed coastal outcrops. Frequent earthquakes and the continued rise above sea level of the islands are further evidence of the undiminished volcanic activity in the region.

When members of Bering's expedition arrived on the islands they found animals and birds they had never seen before. Only Steller's drawings, some bones and the names of some of the capes on the islands – for example, Cape Manatee – recall some of them. The manatees, strange, large, gentle animals, were known as 'Steller's sea cows'. Steller was the first naturalist ever to see these living fossils, and he drew them in detail. His written description of them also survives: 'The largest examples of these animals reach between eight and ten metres in length. Down to the umbilicus it is like a seal, from the umbilicus to the tail it resembles a fish. The skull is not unlike a horse's. It is covered in hair and flesh, with somewhat unusual lips, similar to the head of a buffalo. The eyes of this huge animal are no bigger than sheep's, with no eyelashes. The openings for the ears are small and modest, the ear canal is rather narrow, so that a pea would barely fit inside. There are no signs of any external ear parts. These animals, like cattle, live in the water in herds. They aren't at all afraid of man...Their extraordinary love for one another shows itself in that when one of them is struck, others immediately come to its rescue. They form a circle around the wounded member and guide it away from the shore, whilst others try to overturn the launch boat and lie on the rope in an attempt to pull the harpoon

Bering Island. Inland, the islands have typical mountain tundra landscape, fertile from early summer until later autumn. More than forty varieties of mushroom grow plentifully.

184

The Commander Islands are amongst
the most important sites in the world
for marine seals. Uncontrolled
hunting at the beginning of this
century led to the near-extinction of
many breeds here, but the control
and preservation of the natural
environment of the islands has
helped to re-establish these breeds.

At present there are about three hundred thousand seals on the breeding grounds, and the kalan or sea otter, the most valuable of fur-bearing animals, is under strict protection. There are now eighteen hundred different species of animals and birds on Bering Island and two-and-a-half thousand on Mednyy Island.

Ary Rock. A small rocky islet near
Bering Island, which is densely
populated by birds, the most
common being guillemots, seagulls
and puffins.

Colonies of guillemots crowded
together on bleached and weathered
rocks high above the sea.

from the body...We watched with amazement how for two days the male approached the dead body of its mate lying on the shore, as though enquiring about its condition. But no matter how we tried, or how many we killed, they would not leave this place.' Although an endangered species, manatees can still be found in small numbers in parts of the north Pacific.

Their encounter with man on the Commander Islands, however, was fateful. In 1826 the first commercial hunting settlements appeared on the islands – Preobrazhenskoye on Mednyy Island and Nikolskoye on Bering Island. By then, the population of sea cows had already completely disappeared.

Today, the sandy beach at Commander Bay, where the sailors from the *St Peter* found shelter, still slopes gently down to the sea. It is protected on two sides by reefs, which stretch far out into the ocean and are exposed when the tide goes out. On the shore on a slight rise is an iron cross and a commemorative plaque at the point where Vitus Bering is said to be buried. On landing, our group of four camped in a small tent amongst the clumps of grass, shrubs and driftwood, thrown up by the ocean in stormy weather. Calm weather is rare here, and the next storm is never long in coming. Within a few minutes hurricane-force winds had ripped down our tent poles and we were forced to shelter under damp tarpaulins, held down by heavy logs. The next day was calm and cloudless. The ebb-tide started. The ocean had changed the whole coastline beyond recognition, and, to our great surprise, we found some large, grey bones, for the most part ribs and vertebrae, and heavy as rocks, that had been washed up by the tide. They were the bones of Steller's manatees which had disappeared from the Commander Islands two hundred years ago. The incoming tide quickly covered them, leaving no time to carry even a few of them ashore. We were in no hurry; we could collect them when the tide went out again. The next wind disabused us of this idea. We once more witnessed the rapidly changing face of the coastline. Where yesterday there had been a clear, stony sea floor was a thick sandy covering, small pebbles, and, at the high-water mark, a line of seaweed and driftwood.

188

Seals of many different species rest side-by-side on the beaches of the Commander Islands.

Index